EXILES FROM DIALOGUE

Never to seek the other in the
terrifying illusion of dialogue.
Jean Baudrillard

EXILES FROM DIALOGUE

Jean Baudrillard and Enrique Valiente Noailles

TRANSLATED BY CHRIS TURNER

polity

First published in French as *Les Exilés du dialogue* by Jean Baudrillard and Enrique Valiente Noailles
© Les Éditions Galilée, Paris, 2005.

This English translation © Polity Press, 2007.

Polity Press
65 Bridge Street
Cambridge CB2 1UR, UK

Polity Press
350 Main Street
Malden, MA 02148, USA

Ouvrage publié avec le concours du Ministére français chargé de la culture – Centre National du Livre.

Published with the assistance of the French Ministry of Culture – National Centre for the book

ISBN-13: 978-07456-3990-1
ISBN-13: 978-07456-3991-8 (pb)

A catalogue record for this book is available from the British Library.

Typeset in 11 on 13 pt Sabon
by Servis Filmsetting Ltd, Manchester
Printed and bound in India by Replika Press PVT Ltd, Kundli.

For further information on Polity, visit our website: www.polity.co.uk

Contents

The Retrospective Echo of the Event   3

The *jouissance* of Language   8

The Unbearable Gift   27

The Cloning of God   33

Illusion / Real / Simulation   43

Gradation / Degradation / Hierarchy   58

Transcendence / Immanence   75

The Vaccinated System   79

The Suffering of Stones   88

Neanderthal Man   94

It's the Inhuman that Thinks Us   101

The Genealogy of Disappearance   108

Polychrony   116

The Abolition of Night   120

A Luxurious Dysfunction   130

How to Eat the Nothing?   132

Not long ago, two friends, Jean Baudrillard and Enrique Valiente Noailles, the one having come from Buenos Aires, the other from nowhere, met in Paris. They had a long discussion, without any precise aim. It was more a way of brushing up against metaphysics with no risk of contagion. They gave it the title they did as a mirrored homage to Bertolt Brecht, and shortly afterwards they parted company and went their separate ways.[1]

---

[1] The French title of this work *Les Exilés du Dialogue* is an inversion of *Dialogues d'exilés*, which is the French title of Bertolt Brecht's *Flüchtlingsgespräche* (literally, 'Refugee Conversations'). There are no footnotes in the original work, and such minimal footnotes as have been added in this edition are therefore mine [Trans.].

example, remembers the age of detention: *he is a word* and *then, one day, suddenly begins to speak in order to ask for the sugar. They ask him why he's never spoken before and he says, 'Up until then everything was perfect.' . . . Hence, language is superfluous. This also happens with Mallarmé's poem, where the* one absent *from all bouquets is proof that absence is rest of the* idées . . . *we decipher into language.*

It's roughly the same with the world. The world is perfect if you take it as it is in its absolute coherence. Then that coherence is disturbed until you have so much of explain it, weave it, recreate – and that's the beginning of the conflict . . .

. . . It is that idea . . . a perfectly operational world where everything functions smoothly, a world that no longer needs *us*, a world from which we would be *absent*.

You have to restore to language its perfection; it's perfect and recondant at one and the same time. As, indeed, is the eternally unresolved sentence of John Berger: the sugar question. In John's case, the perfection precedes language – as if it were almost the realisation of the end of history. In another, language resisted, perhaps waited, till the end of the process. With everything in stable technologically in a perfectly operational world, there will, once again, be no need to speak. And John, who won't ask for anything – even sugar – will fall silent again. The fully accomplished world will be the end of language. The quest for a perfect world and a perfect language . . . total information, total coherence: the quest that haunts our present world, is then, perfectly . . . , but you can also take the view that perfection is an assymptote, a world merely playing at . . .

The Retrospective Echo of the Event

ENRIQUE VALIENTE NOAILLES: *I'd like to begin our conversation by referring to Giorgio Manganelli, the Italian writer. He says he believes in God, but that God himself is an atheist . . .*

JEAN BAUDRILLARD: If God doesn't believe in God, perhaps he's never existed. Like reality. It exists only if you believe in it. But perhaps reality doesn't believe in it itself. If put on a lie-detector, it would perhaps admit it doesn't exist.

And if it existed, it would more likely be polytheistic! . . . But Manganelli also says: 'It's possible that a ticking, coming from somewhere, simulates

3

thought and marks hours that don't yet exist and have never begun.' I find that a little bit of a metaphor for your work: a ticking that comes ahead of the clock. It could, of course, also be the ticking of the timing device on a bomb!

Yes. In any case, time itself is a time bomb.

Yes, it seems a thinker is at once a kind of anticipation of an age and the precipitation of that age towards its end. That might be the case with you. What do you think?

It isn't so much a question of anticipation; that's still within a classical dimension of linear prediction. It isn't an anticipated verification either. If you say, 'I've been saying it was coming for a long time and there you are, it's happened!', then you're verifying your own thought, but fulfilled prophecy robs the event of its singularity. What you have there is merely the image-feedback of thought on the event. The problem is, rather, that of a precession of thought over the event – and yet, simultaneously, of the precession of the event over thought. It's this double helix that's mysterious. In the case of the World Trade Center, for example, everything I've been writing for twenty years was, ultimately, something like a prefigured shock wave of the event, as though it had always been there, identified in a kind of retrospective anticipation. Thought's neither a prophecy nor a prediction. It's a prefiguration. It's already there like the event in a sense, and it finds its fulfilment in something that wholly escapes it. The event impacts on thought even before it has occurred. And when it finally happens, it's both the realization of thought and its end.

The event might be said to take place at several places at once, then, without any previous history. Thought and event would be face to face – not like mirrors, but like strange attractors. Between them you might say there's a secret correspondence, a silent pact, like the pact between two parallel lines that would agree to meet somewhere one day. Something particularly interesting also follows from what you say: it would perhaps be one of thought's additional tasks not to get in the way of the singularity of the event, as well as to protect that singularity from the assault of any reductive transcription. Perhaps part of its effort consists in deterring the artificial, premature production of the event. At any rate, it seems to me there is in thought a jouissance *and an expectation where the idea of precipitation is concerned. Borges said, 'Almost immediately, reality collapsed at several points – the truth is that it wanted to give way.' It's as though reality were waiting for something that would precipitate it, and thought procured that pleasure for it. In this sense, for example, there was a kind of implosion of the concept of 'the social' after* In the Shadow of the Silent Majorities[2] *– without any direct causality, of course.*

The appearance of thought itself is of the order of an event. In that sense, it brings things more quickly to a head. That something like 'the social' is hurtling towards its end – and that the analysis of the social contributes to that – is certain. It's more or less the story of the river speeding up as it comes to the waterfall. All things speed up once they've lost their principle. History, they say, is accelerating. In fact, history has disappeared, but it's left the acceleration behind. We might, in the same way, say reality has disappeared, but it's

---

[2] J. Baudrillard, *In the Shadow of the Silent Majorities* (New York: Semiotext[e], 1983). Original French edition: *A l'ombre des majorités silencieuses* (Fontenay-sous-Bois: Cahiers d'Utopie, 1978).

left us its principle. Or the reality principle has disappeared, but it's left us reality. It's marvellous, this reality that speeds up like a headless chicken, while its principle goes on like a chickenless head. There are other parallel patterns: God himself, who has disappeared, but has left us his judgement that still hovers over us like the grin of the famous Cheshire Cat in *Alice in Wonderland*.

Yes, we're left with just the worst residues! Perhaps what's currently being lost calls on thought to help speed up the process. We might think of thought as being always on standby to do this, as well as to lay bare everything that's lost its principle. But your work perhaps goes further: like a neutron bomb, it leaves the pure literality of objects standing while it vaporizes their foundations. There's an abrupt neutralization of meaning in that 'operation', but at bottom it's merely the neutralization of the attempt to neutralize the world. In a way, you do a 'Suite vénitienne' on the world itself, without seeking to take its secret from it: shadowing it and following it in order to wipe away its traces from afar and abolish it.[3]

You can widen this out to the world. 'Shadowing the world' is following the world like its shadow, while at the same time stealing its identity. A distant echo of Peter Schlemihl, the man who lost his shadow, but here the lost shadow comes back again to dog its steps. Once they've been followed like this and shorn of their shadows, things no longer have any precise ends. All functions, set free from their goals, their ends, their use-values in this way, become exponential. That's how it is with reality: set free from its principle, it invades everything and goes off in any direction.

[3] 'Suite vénitienne' is the title of a 'photo essay' by Sophie Calle on the obsessive surveillance of a passing acquaintance, identified as Henri B., over a thirteen-day period in Venice in 1981.

Yes. To put it another way, thought's not beyond things, but before them, so to speak. It comes before things are constituted in themselves, before they're petrified in an irreversible logic of causal order and linear temporality. It's an act of prestidigitation by which you pull away the tablecloth leaving the objects on the table, because there's always a material presence of objects, from which, however, the meaning has been removed.

That's right. Or taking things by surprise before the tablecloth has been laid. This is how it had seemed to me with the photographic object: to arrive even before the objects had entered the order of reference. As soon as you're present, you give them a meaning, and it's already too late. So, you have to take advantage of the little space of time when you're still not really there, take advantage of your absence to grasp what the world may be in your absence.

Yes, because when things notice you're there, they take on reality or, to go on with the photographic image, they begin to pose in the light of meaning. It's important not just that they don't realize you're there, but even that we ourselves don't manage to notice our own presence too much either. For us not to, thought must preserve a furtiveness in its movement.

The act of thought is, in fact, furtive. Like the photographic act, it's an act of disappearance. An act in which you eclipse yourself at the same time as you capture things.

Perhaps thought, in a first phase, strikes a pact of reflection and symmetry with the movement of the world, only to eclipse itself immediately afterwards by prompting the world, by reflection, to behave in the same way. It's prompted, then, to take part in an asymmetrical duel, a duel of mutual furtiveness. The problem of the real and its petrification is that it shows only a single phase of things, the phase of appearance. Thought consigns them once again to disappearance.

It means restoring an absence that is usually dispelled by a total presence. Starting out from the idea that events all want to come to pass, but are obstructed by meaning and history, you have to remove everything in the event's way, to disobstruct it by creating a void – to take things out of the confines of their reality, to wrest reality from the reality principle.

The *jouissance* of Language

NOAILLES: *I'd like to speak a little about writing and language. At one stage, you used terms like 'symbolic exchange', 'fatefulness', 'seduction', 'hyperreality', etc. Your work seems to have explored all the resources of language and now expresses itself in a manner beyond metaphor and closer to absolute literalness. How, retrospectively, do you see your relation to language?*

BAUDRILLARD: The concepts from the early days still belong to conventional language. They're the common repertoire of the disciplines that were prevalent at the time: anthropology, semiology, psychoanalysis . . . , but with a requirement to deconstruct them. Or, rather, not deconstruct them, but take the terms to their limits, show up their emptiness. To make them disqualify themselves in order to open up other issues. It was at that point that simulacrum, seduction, the hyperreal and the fateful [*le fatal*] appeared: terms not substitutable for one another, but succeeding each other and unfolding in a kind of spiral. At any rate, at that point theoretical language stopped being conceptual, and the very form became a challenge to objective signification. Nothing operated in an equivalent or dialectical relation any longer, but, by a kind of escalation, language became a fatal strategy [*stratégie fatale*]. It was no longer an instrument of the production of meaning, but of appearance and disappearance, imposing its own surprises, events and catastrophes. And, in the end, in fact, what there is here is a kind of material articulation of language, a literalness that has its own rules. This is true even of theoretical language: it's no longer exactly that we impose ideas on it. What we mean is what we say, but it's also what *it* wants to say – 'it sometimes happens that words, through his mouth, say true and profound things' (Schnitzler).

The danger, the classical short-sighted objection, is to say you're producing literature, or poetry.

There's a risk of that, but what you have to avoid, above all, is labour and boredom. You mustn't weary language, you mustn't force it to say what it doesn't want to. Even if you have your own idea, you have to avoid making language suffer. And it's a question of rhythm.

They sometimes say that people are crushed or depressed by what you write. For my part, I get great delight [jouissance] *from reading you.*

That's the idea. Writing's neither alternative nor redemptive. Nihilistic or not (it may be so in content, but never in form), it always offers a bonus of *jouissance*. The pleasure of writing is in the form. But are people truly sensitive to the *form* of writing? And to the distance it maintains from what it says? That distance in itself is a *jouissance*. Are people sensitive to the implicit seductiveness of what's left unsaid? They're generally sensitive only to the content, to the expression of the ideas. But the only thing that counts is the form the ideas assume, and whether that form is a felicitous one. Sadly, most of the time those who write just add infelicity of form to infelicity of content.

Yes, in more recent writing, there might be said to be a form equivalent to what you call integral reality. An 'integral writing' that never knows how to stop what it's saying before it's said, the expression of which goes right to the end of what it has to say, thereby rendering any reading superfluous. A form that shapes ideas brutally, just as integral reality pushes the real to the point of brutality; that uses language as a recipient into which to pour the content of what you have to say, instead of letting language form a mimetic relation, as it were, with its content, so that the two lend each other added force. We're talking about a writing that is entirely profane in its relation to language, but is, above all, sad, like everything that exhausts meaning. Lastly, it's utterly boring, as you were saying. A writing oriented towards jouissance *seems to be a style whose main achievement is to surprise language itself. Perhaps* jouissance *has to do with effecting the disruption of thought in the face of the total de-realization of the world. This freeing-up of thought, this freedom to think the world the other way round – perhaps that's where* jouissance *lies.*

Yes, and at the same time the fact of rediscovering symbolic chains. The fact, with the free circulation of ideas in full swing, of rediscovering an obligation;

the fact, amid a total permissiveness of meaning, of rediscovering the material chaining of forms and language. Where you come back to the – immoral and poetic – maxim of Omar Khayyam: 'One freeman whom thy kindness has enslaved / Outweighs by far a thousand slaves set free.'[4] The extreme deregulation (liberalization) of the world forces us to invent another set of rules, to play on reversibility, to enter into a 'fatal strategy' of inversion, into a poetic transference of situation. And that too is a source of *jouissance*.

The search for this chaining [enchaînement], *language in pursuit of a new restriction of meaning, reminds me also of that fine line from Kafka's* Diaries: *'A cage went out in search of a bird.' The tender nature of that pursuit chimes with the idea of chaining up something with kindness. Language seems to be a form in search of a content that would be sufficiently seduced to chain itself up voluntarily. There's a kind of autonomy of language in writing. It isn't language that obeys, but language that controls the situation, and you have to let it say what it has to say.*

Yes, all contents have been liberated, but nobody can liberate language as form. You never liberate a form; it's the form that enchains you. Hence all these inverted formulas: it's the object that thinks us; it's language that thinks us; it's the world that thinks us – formulas of duality and reversibility.

And of a kind of adequation to the very form of language, of respect for the form of appearance and disappearance of language.

[4] Omar Khayyam, quoted from Reynold A. Nicholson, *The Mystics of Islam* (London: Routledge & Kegan Paul, 1914).

It's a perpetual dramaturgy, but you mustn't, above all, fall into the formal trap of language: form has to remain an inner challenge; it mustn't appear as an ideal solution. It's like the figure in the carpet, its outline must remain secret.

On the other hand, there is in the delight in reading and writing a kind of coupling between pleasure and violence, as you suggest in Cool Memories.[5] *If there's no violence, there's no pleasure. It isn't a question of any old violence or any old pleasure. These aren't either the sort of violence or pleasure that would have a positive reference from which to extract their* jouissance: *their source of* jouissance *is linked to the volatilization of the referent in the very act of naming it. It's this form of precisely calibrated destruction that provides language with a permanent blood transfusion. In this way, for example, the poetic, as the paradigm of language, may be said to act as a protective atmosphere: it breaks up meaning when meaning, after the manner of meteorites, attempts to pass through it. The work of language could be said to lie in withdrawal, in what it leaves behind when it withdraws, like that fine phrase of Hölderlin's: 'God created the world by withdrawing.'*

That's right. The violence writing does to its own content, the charm of the exasperation of language and that of the violence done to meaning, that of thwarting meaning in its very expression. The enigma of meaning is the secret of writing, and this is expressed in its concision and its aphoristic form. I would like, for example, to have made an anthology of short, elliptical phrases that seemed to me to entrap meaning, all possible meanings, in a subtle twist. This one, for example: 'There isn't a woman in the world

[5] Jean Baudrillard, *Cool Memories* (London: Verso, 1990).

12

whose possession would be more precious than the truth she reveals to you by making you suffer.'[6] That simple sentence is inexhaustible. Or this one: 'Existence isn't everything. It is, even, the least of things.' As Rimbaud said, that is 'true literally and in all senses'. Interpretation has no purchase on it. Or this other one: 'Death resists us. It does its best, but it gives in in the end.' This is beyond our imagining, but it's the finest thing that can be said about death. It's by Stanislaw Lec. It's the only way of conquering death, the idea of death, and giving it back to us as something almost intimate and familiar.

If I can just add two or three sentences to these, though not in the same sense, sentences that render a pure power of language, without the least meaning becoming clear in them, though without meaning being absent either. 'Powdered water: just add water to get water.'[7] That's marvellous. It's difficult to go further. Or again: 'He was so thin he had to pass the same spot twice to cast a shadow.' That's a linguistic delight. A third one, by the Chilean poet Vicente Huidobro: 'The four points of the compass are three: North and South.' There's genius in this compression of meaning, this rapidity, this electrocution of language . . . What can you add to that?

It's a little bit what we could say of Rothko and his work, which opens up and closes in all directions at one and the same time – it's unassailable. This seems to me to be characteristic of every singularity: impregnable from outside and totally open towards the inside – initiatory. Such sentences are more precious than a whole explanatory presentation. They are, by their

---

[6] Jean Baudrillard, *Cool Memories IV, 1995–2000* (London: Verso, 2003), p. 117.
[7] Jean Baudrillard, *Cool Memories I*, p. 69.

transparent opacity, a kind of miracle, since they have behind them, nonetheless, a clandestine intuition of meaning. It isn't nonsense; it's just before meaning arrives; before the trap closes again.

Yes, it seems the clandestine character of language and that of thought and the world intersect for a moment. It's a one-off, luminous revelation, without any possible development. And the jouissance *lies perhaps in the movement of withdrawal at the same moment as it appears. This fits with what you've said: 'Language expatriates itself into words that are afraid to signify.'*

Perhaps too this ellipsis is the sacrificial aspect of language, the sacrificial aspect of thought. Poems too are elliptical in the literal sense (*ek-leipein*) in which they leave all the rest outside and are sufficient in themselves. They're not closed in the sense of being closed to the world, but in the sense that there's nothing beyond the horizon of the poem. They are, in that sense, initiatory. The poem is the microcosm. It exhausts all its possibilities in itself, and, as a result, what does it leave you? It leaves you *jouissance*. It doesn't leave you the possibility of escaping *jouissance* by meaning. But the violence of interpretation, there as everywhere, is always ready to re-establish order and to forbid us *jouissance*. And, indeed, most things deserve nothing but commentary.

Escaping jouissance *by meaning – I like that expression. Perhaps, then, the whole immense process of the destruction of the world through meaning comes from a secret terror of* jouissance? *This suspicion is corroborated by the fact that the most frequent and emphatic declaration of human beings, from Aristotle onwards, concerns the pursuit of happiness. It's possible that*

the avowal of this pursuit of joy is a cloak concealing the actual path taken,
which runs in the opposite direction. Beneath this declaration of principle,
the opposite form is playing itself out, a form of horror, the construction of
an igloo of meaning to protect ourselves from jouissance. *(However, just as*
the destruction of the world through meaning has the aim of ridding itself of
a form of jouissance, *so perhaps this whole opposite thrust of the destruc-*
tion of meaning is linked to its recovery.) After all, what reason would we
have to protect ourselves from jouissance *by taking refuge in the realization*
of the world and the destruction of illusion? Perhaps because a fundamental
aspect of jouissance *is that you can't store it up (in the same way as you can't*
save up anything from a felicitous phrase), and misfortune is preferred for
its 'hoardable' character! Jouissance *can only be seduced, but misfortune can*
be produced.

That's true. There's no remainder, no residue, either in the poem or in *jouis-*
sance. The event is total, but it's finite. It's like the sphere of play – a field
circumscribed by rules and in itself unassailable. But we mustn't idealize
play against the real, since the form of play is not opposed to the real. There
are two almost diametrically opposed routes for liquidating the real and
meaning. I think we should speak in the one case (the virtual) of an irrevo-
cable extermination and in the other of a playing with meaning, with its disappearance, a perpetual thwarting of meaning, not its denial. Play isn't a
denial of the real. It doesn't put an end to it. It makes sport of it, in the same
way as seduction sports with desire. It's a form of appearance/disappearance,
not a radical elimination.

Perhaps it's difficult not to fall into the temptation of torturing meaning, in
response to the torture it inflicts. But you're right, since to play against the

real is to remain absolutely captive to – and, ultimately, complicit with – the real itself, by reflection, as in the aleatory, 'artistic' or surrealistic rupture. It's the same with the distinction you make: not sub-version, but reversion.

Play isn't opposed to anything. You can say of play, as you can of the nothing, that it's perfect because it's not opposed to anything. We should look, rather, towards radical exoticism (Segalen) or the magical abstraction of that singular object, the fetish.

How might we describe the fetish?

Though the fetishism of commodities, which characterizes the abstract circulation of all values, is fascinating, let's leave it aside and look at the fetish object. According to Freud, it's the substitute object for the sexual relation. So it's no more sexual in itself than the fetishized commodity is a material object. It's an abstract prosthesis, a kind of disembodied mental object – an article of clothing, a shoe, a jewel, an accessory – in which the impossible exchange of sex is gathered and crystallized. It is, if you like, an idol, but it's no longer a sign. It's meaningless in itself, but it takes the place of everything. Of everything that cannot take place. Which means that it can't be exchanged for anything. It is, in a sense, a pure object – an artefact, an artifice (this is the literal sense of the word 'fetish'). It's the perfect sex object since it substitutes for any real sex, just as the abstraction of the commodity substitutes for any exchange of real goods, just as virtual reality substitutes for the real world and thereby becomes the form of our modern fetishism. A radical fetishism this, since it affects all areas of existence and knowledge.

We may say all the new technologies have become our new object of desire (I wouldn't venture to say 'perverse' object, as Freud has it with his definition of fetishism as perversion). More generally, there's fetishism when there's no longer transference of meaning, no longer any possible metaphor, when the object merges with the operation of the sign. As with the man who jumps into the dustcart shouting, 'I'm rubbish!', for example; or Harpo Marx who, wanting to get into a club that has 'swordfish' as its password, turns up with a swordfish under his arm. It's literalness that upsets the operation of the sign.

Or the woman who sends her eyes to the lover who has praised them. 'If you like them so much . . .'

Yes, she too has lost the sense of metaphor. But, with her, it's a deliberate sacrifice and a poetic act of defiance. The lover must have been crushed by that absolute gift.

Absolute literalness.

And totally cruel. The lover having fetishized her gaze, she gives him her eyes as literal object. You can see the magical element in fetishism, in this electrocution of meaning and metaphor.

She'd lost the sense of metaphor, but she'd perhaps gained the sense of metonymy! She'd chosen to stay outside the system of representation to carry out an operation of pure contiguity. In another register, it reminds me of the story of the pirate who threw all his vanquished enemies into the sea one by one, after first asking each his name. One of them, a crafty sailor, replied with the name of the pirate standing before him: the blood-thirsty Jacob Cow. The terror inspired by the name was so great that the real Jacob Cow went back to his ship and vanished. He might well have thrown himself into the sea![8] *The terror belonged to the name itself, independently of its bearer, and circulated in something like a chain reaction, an abstract substitution. You might say that in the collection of phrases we've just cited, there's also an absolute literalness. But everything's open in it, whereas in the pure object, everything's closed.*

Yes, it's a definitive response that closes off the game through amputation of the sign and a literal short-circuiting. It's the equivalent of the joke in language. The *Witz*, too, is a use of the literalness of language that explodes meaning. Many things in there are of the order of humour, of a savage humour – for example, the sacrifice the woman makes of her eyes by taking her suitor's conventional homage literally.

Kant said laughter was an affection arising out of the sudden transformation of a strained expectation into nothing. Humour relieves us and delivers us perhaps from what we hope for . . . But that isn't the whole secret of the operation, because it isn't just any old 'transformation . . . into nothing'. It isn't just anything colliding with just anything.

---

[8] This story comes from Jean Paulhan's *Jacob Cow le pirate ou Si les mots sont des signes* (Paris: Au Sans Pareil, 1921), where it is ascribed to Pierre MacOrlan.

No, of course not. It isn't a Brownian collision of particles. And, indeed, it's the weakness of a rearguard aesthetic, a gimcrack Surrealism, that any old kinds of thing are brought together. You find this sort of random manipulation and creativity everywhere. There's no happy coincidence any longer; there's just a promiscuity of everything, an obscene contiguity. It's a wholesale exploitation of chance, begun, in fact, by the Surrealists with their *hasard objectif*. Breaking down the traditional order of things was a fine programme, but if it's to end up in a generalized probability, a reintensified promiscuity, so to speak – that is to say, the opposite of a fateful order, the order of happy coincidences – then the poetic project has collapsed. The same error is made by the 'dice man' in his plan to entrust all his decisions to chance. That's just a random 'devolution' – a veritable parody of fate which, for its part, is based not on random selection, but on elective affinities, and on a rigorous coincidence between will and event. In the fateful order, the will must coincide obscurely with what befalls you. Merely removing the will by throwing dice isn't enough to gain you a destiny, just as saying anything whatever isn't enough to make you enigmatic.

Yes, for there to be a poetic effect, for there to be a happy coincidence, there has to be absolute necessity – even at the level of language or the level of the pure object and the event. An acknowledgement of necessity, not of chance.

Absolutely not of chance. Chance is a derivative, a by-product of the rational, causal world. Instead of a rational enchainment, what you have there is a rational unchaining, in which everything is jumbled, in which everything can be the cause of anything. Now, this is the absolute danger: this kind of mixing, hybridization, confusion and generalized exchange that we're given to believe is a liberation of things. Multiculturalism, multimedia, interactivity – so many watchwords of a false revolution of desire. Though doubtless not false in fact: the ideal of liberation is that everything should communicate with everything else; it's generalized exchange, prefigured on the global scale by economic liberalism. Now, there's a fundamental rule in the symbolic order that keeps things apart. If you break that rule, then everything comes into interaction, in an unbridled immanence. But there's no source of *jouissance* in this any longer – except in the sense of a mere thrill at a chain reaction. So the play of the virtual and of multiple identities is a form of transitional activity in which you rediscover a little of the infantile confusion, of the virtual omnipotence of thought Freud spoke of, in which language hasn't yet assumed the force of a symbolic obligation – an informal stage which is also, in my opinion, the stage of information, in its profusion and confusion. And there is, indeed, an intense satisfaction in that, a collective satisfaction that might be said to be of the order of desire if the word still had a meaning.

How, then, are we to distinguish this morbid and exponential jouissance *of infinite commutation from the* jouissance *that attaches to a rigorous necessity and to the singular form of the poetic?*

In the sexual order, the exponential downhill path would be that of homogenization and the extenuation of difference. This is the general watchword: everything tends towards transsexuality, towards a total sexual plasticity and flexibility, beyond sexual difference properly so-called. But it's the opposite of seduction which, for its part, is far beyond sexual multiplicity. Seduction might be said to correspond to the maximum degree of *jouissance*, whereas the unlimited play of sex, while equating to a performance (Catherine Millet), would equate also to the zero degree of *jouissance*. It's on this basis that transsexuality, which was formerly a psychotic hallucination, has become one of our human rights (should we conclude from this that human rights have become a psychotic hallucination?). Seduction, for its part, will never be part of human rights. Sex is, ultimately, merely a reductive hypothesis in relation to seduction, and transsexuality an even more reductive hypothesis in relation to sexuality itself. Perhaps the final solution. The extremization of sex as minimum degree of sex, so to speak.

It's always the same: absolute disorder or seduction. When there's an effect of jouissance, *you don't pass through the second instance, do you, but jump directly from the first to the third?*

That's right. Through sex, you find yourself up against the impossible exchange of sex and, in just the opposite way, on the seduction side of things, you get back to a form of impossible exchange. *Jouissance* of generalized exchange, *jouissance* of impossible exchange. It's both homologous and entirely antithetical.

It's the same with Zen, which says: 'Before studying Zen, the mountains are mountains and the rivers are rivers. During the learning of Zen, the mountains are no longer mountains and the rivers are no longer rivers. Once you've learned Zen, the mountains are mountains and the rivers are rivers.' Between the first and the third instances, things are radically different, but you state them in the same way. When you say, 'The mountains are mountains and the rivers are rivers,' then perhaps, in Heideggerian terms, what you understand by 'being' isn't the same thing. 'Being' in the first instance is a kind of petrified identity, while 'being' in the third instance is a total

21

openness (perhaps the openness that opens and closes in all directions, as you said of Rothko). Perhaps the expression zero degree/maximum degree represents the difficulty of putting the two phenomena on a single scale discursively. From one reduction to the next (sex against seduction and transsexuality against sex), it would seem that you reach the end of a process, whereas what's going on is perhaps a pure reversion without these things lying on any shared scale. And this reversion would be a way of understanding the Zen figure: the reversion of the third stage precisely never belongs to the class of the negation of the second. This difference even justifies the appearance of this second stage, which does the work of absorbing all the energy of negation and excludes it from the other instances. Could we establish a consonance between our Zen example and these lines of Hölderlin, even if we had to put the word 'truth' in inverted commas? 'For once between Day and Night must / A truth be made manifest. / Now three-fold circumscribe it, / Yet unuttered also, just as you found it, / Innocent virgin, let it remain.'[9]

I don't know what figurative representation you can give to this; the two extremes of the mountain meet. In the one, it's a mountain assured of its existence, in the other it's merely a paradoxical moment that revives at every instant. Perhaps we could see it as the figure of the *ouroboros*, the creature that bites its own tail and encircles the whole world before looping back on itself. And to this topology I'd like to add the Moebius strip, another interesting figure, in which each surface becomes its reverse on a continuous band. There's no confusion between the one and the other, yet there is transfusion. Isn't that reversibility and, at the same time, the end of the dialectic,

[9] Hölderlin, 'Germania', trans. Michael Hamburger in Eric L. Santner (ed.), *Hyperion and Selected Poems* (New York: Continuum, 1990), p. 215.

since the reverse becomes the obverse, the positive becomes the negative (and vice versa) without a blow having been struck? There's no difference any more, but transference. No logical or dialectical opposition, but a curving, an involution of the world into itself.

Encircling the whole world and then looping back on itself cancels out any difference between origin and end: everything is closed and open at the same time. These figures say more than any attempt to make the world signify . . .

'Signifying' is of our invention, as is the order of 'causing to do'. The virtual is causing and causing-to-do; information is making known, causing-to-know; communication is making speak, causing-to-speak; advertising is causing-to-be-valued. These things are all factitive and perhaps even factitious; they're simulation in action, the operational, the place where everything *changes*, but nothing *becomes*.

The strategy of opposition: if we mustn't play off truth against truth, we mustn't play off total liberation against truth either – all that's needed is a slight manipulation of appearances as you were saying. Between the banal and the fateful, there's just this slight difference in the manipulation of appearances. It's like the 'signifying' we were just talking about: the poetic doesn't signal to liberation, nor to the accomplishment of the world, it merely gives a little nod and a wink.

I'd even say that it creates a new pact, a total complicity with appearances, without any obligation to truth. I think of Hölderlin again when he speaks of rivers, trees, cities and mythical heroes. He doesn't speak of them in mythological terms at all, in allegorical or romantic terms. He's the site of their dramaturgy. He's the place where the gods metamorphose, the place where rivers metamorphose, the site where all the fragments of becoming converge. He doesn't liberate the world, he doesn't express it. He's at the confluence of the forces that come from all sides, and he's in thrall to their metamorphosis. You find this in Rimbaud too, from *Illuminations* to *A Season in Hell*: it's a continual metamorphosis from one sentence to the next, and the form conveys this surprise of the whole world in a few sentences.

As in Fragment 12 of Heraclitus ('As they step into the same rivers, other and still other waters flow upon them'). There's a symbiosis between what he says and the way he says it; the river and the flow are in the rhythm of the language . . . And, to come back to Rimbaud, he seems to efface himself in the language . . .

He's the absent site, the site of the succession of appearances.

This is perhaps one of the ways his 'I is another' can be taken?

If the 'I' identifies with itself, it's a one-way complicity. It is what it is, and the other is merely the residue. True alterity is what you become, never what you are. What you are is merely the object of alienation.

A fine age, the age of alienation!

Yes, and we're currently losing that too, along with criticism and negation. Soon we'll be able to look back on all that as a golden age.

A nostalgia syndrome? We might even say that when the real is being denigrated, we see a kind of dynamism of the mirage: reality shifts, but the lost paradise does so at the same pace.

Yes, with the upsurge of the global, it's universal values that come to seem like a golden age and a lost paradise. Reality, at the moment of its disappearance, becomes part of the heritage of the species, something akin to a human right . . . a democratic value, a value to be defended. All the values of the nineteenth century are buffed up and revalorized to protect ourselves from apprehending the present world in panic mode. There's always regression, as in Freud's sexual mechanism of fetishism, to the immediately preceding stage.

Towards the paroxystic object, the one that protects you from the end . . .

As we speak of the transitional object, the one that leads to reality, so the paroxystic object (in the literal sense *par-oxyton* means 'penultimate', 'the one before last') is the one that precedes the end, that's just before the end. It's different, then, from the customary meaning as the 'last' or 'culminating moment'.

There's an antagonistic connection here between language and perfection. Language never coincides with perfection; we might even say it comes at the point where perfection ceases to be. As in the wonderful story of John, for example, who reaches the age of 14 without saying a word and then, one day, suddenly begins to speak in order to ask for the sugar. They ask him why he's never spoken before and he says, 'Up until then, everything was perfect' . . . Hence, language was superfluous. This also happens with Mallarmé's poetic flower, the 'one absent from all bouquets'; without that absence the rest of the flowers are de trop, *as is language.*

It's roughly the same with the world. The world is perfect if you take it as it is, as absolute self-evidence. Then that self-evidence is disturbed, and you have to begin to explain it, to give it a meaning – and that's the beginning of the end.

It's what Nietzsche called 'amor fati'. In other words, there's only one possibility: that of accepting the world tragically.

You have to restore to it its criminal perfection, since it's perfect and criminal at one and the same time. As, indeed, is the entirely abnormal existence of John before the sugar episode. In John's case, the perfection preceding language is idyllic; it's almost the perfection of the state of nature. But another criminal perfection perhaps awaits us at the end of the process. With everything available technologically in a perfectly operational world, there will, once again, be no need to speak. And John, who won't lack for anything, even sugar, will fall dumb again. The fully accomplished world will be the end of language. The quest for a perfect world and a perfect human being, for total information and total efficiency, the quest that haunts our present world, is, then, perfectly criminal. But you can also take the view that perfection's merely a game, that we're merely playing at arriving at an ultimate point, a terminal point, with the idea that it will never end there and that the movement will always take us beyond the end. We may even hypothesize that we've reached that point already, that we're already beyond the end, beyond perfection, and in the failure that inevitably follows or, even, that accompanies it like a double. There's always a moment when the sugar runs out. And what's thrilling is this moment when the perfection of the real falters, in the convulsions of perfection itself and in its final failure. Moreover, in this strange topology, we must correct an error: that of believing that the failure comes at the end of the perfection. It is there from the outset and follows perfection like its shadow. From the beginning, we're beyond the end. The two processes get under way at the same time, like the Big Bang and the Big Crunch in the theory of the double arrow of time, like life and death. They're born and grow at the same time, contrary to the illusion of death coming at the end of life. All processes trigger the opposing process as soon as they begin, and the story of John is a myth: there never has been an ideal moment, the moment of perfection, when there was no lack of sugar.

The Unbearable Gift

NOAILLES: *One's always rediscovering the difference between this kind of originary perfection, an absolute response to what is there from the outset, and the 'other' perfection, the one you look for at the end.*

BAUDRILLARD: You're quite right, but, once again, the perfection of the beginning is mythic, allegorical, and that of the end is nowhere to be found.

Neither is bearable. We're wrenched from the former by language, and we resist the latter by language. And why are we so mortally allergic to perfection, which we otherwise claim to be our ideal? Doubtless because we can't bear the world being perfect without us; because then we're excluded from it. And yet, in a perverse way, it's the destiny we're manufacturing for ourselves: a perfectly operational world from which we'll automatically be excluded as human beings – while believing we're creating a world in our image.

Hypotheses that are both fine and fearsome: the hypothesis of jealousy towards what unfolds better without us, and that of resentment against what we perceive as lacking nothing, and particularly against all that we perceive as having no need of us. Excluded from the beginning, we've adopted the destruction of this world as destiny, so as to perish like Samson bringing his temple down around him. There is, however, no human force that can demolish the world, which is why we've intuited a more subtle form of destruction that is within our grasp: its duplication. The hypothesis of the virtual.

Exactly. Ultimately, we could take this (technology, simulation, the virtual) as a challenge to the natural perfection of the given world, a challenge to God who gave it to us, if you like – going back, by way of that metaphor, to the fundamental symbolic rule, which states that the unilateral gift is unbearable and that all giving must be reciprocated. There is, then, no original innocence, and the world as it is isn't innocent. It's a poisoned chalice, and we can't accept it as that. We can't take responsibility for it either, because the debt would be too onerous. And yet it's God's strategy to make us responsible for it, or to redeem the debt (or to pretend to do so by the sacrifice of his son), which puts us even more in his debt and overwhelms us even more. We have, then, to dispel this natural world and respond with a world made by our own hand, a world desired and designed by us. The true response lies in defiant challenge, not at all in the idea of being 'free' or 'responsible'. It's in the challenge that the responsibility is total, and that it's resolved. In this sense, the enterprise of substituting a world made with our own hands for a given world is, indeed, a metaphysical challenge and one that conforms, in some way, to the symbolic rule (one always has to bear this in mind in the critical evaluation of technology). The unfortunate thing is that this operation implies a substitution for the natural human being of an artificial, inhuman being, the future sovereign of this virtual universe, born of an endless duel with the natural world. In this sense, too, the virtual is a form of disappearance, but that disappearance is, at least, one we shall have desired.

This counter-gift makes us dependent on the original giver. That is perhaps the way God ensures the impossibility of any atheism, in Nietzsche's sense: i.e. as freedom from debts (Un-schuld) *to the gods. This is the reason for the rush to have original sin exist, for such haste to be finished with innocence. This search for reciprocity with God by means of this cruel, sacrificial exorcism of the world is a curious thing. Is it a question of dismantling it and duplicating it every inch of the way, by seeking out the original tracks of God? Is it a dissimulated extermination that conceals the shame of its own cruelty? Is it a question of gaining a counter-*jouissance *from our own suffering? Anything goes, except not responding at all, which would in a sense be worse than the virtual realization, wouldn't it?*

It would mean losing face, which is worse than death. This symbolic rule, which has very largely been lost in the free circulation of things, is, nonetheless, absolute. I don't know if the world in its primal, raw state obeys it, but in the human order everything operates in terms of this rule – without it having to be reflected upon or internalized.

It's an obligation overarching all rational calculations. We say, ignorance of the law is no excuse. But, in fact, we are ignorant, we can be ignorant, of the law. On the other hand, secretly no one's ignorant of this rule, and no one transgresses it. The whole technical and scientific enterprise should be analysed in these terms: is it a massive response, a gigantic counter-gift, or does it attempt definitively to break this symbolic rule?

That's a tremendous perspective! It remains only to work out what God himself is responding to in 'giving back' this world! What did he receive before he gave it back? In our case, the world is given back as we received it, doubly realized by us.

Yes, redoubled by artifice – it's a fatal strategy of the artefact. And this changes the coloration of things, because it goes beyond a mere critique of technology. What's at stake? What are the symbolic stakes in all this?

What is happening seems, in fact, to be part not of a moral process of becoming, but of a symbolic one. Taking the term 'symbolic' in its etymological sense,[10] the whole act of the duplication of the world seems to be

---

[10] In Greek the word σύμβολον, which derives from συμβάλλειν (to reunite), refers to the two halves of a token that are broken and reunited.

a despair at the absence of one half, that half which, if it coincided or fitted, would make it possible to recognize the totality. We might be said, then, to be producing that half artificially. As a result, this evolution/ involution can no longer be read in terms of denigration or approbation: ultimately, as you say, the issue extends far beyond a banal critique of technology.

You can judge all the consequences of technology negatively, but from this other point of view there's no longer either negative or positive. It is, rather, a wager. This is played out within a dual relation, not the framework of an objective reality. Seen from this angle, all the ideas of technical progress, of positive transformation of the world, are swept away. The management of reality, all the internal developments of technology and science become, so to speak, a by-product. What's essential is going on elsewhere and no one's fully in control.

Perhaps there's also an obligation to manufacture a perfection equal to the perfection we take ourselves to have received. A kind of obligation to put ourselves in God's place.

That's the idea of a rivalry with God, rather than a religious obligation (here again religion masks the more radical dual relation), the idea of an ever-open challenge rather than a division of tasks. An irresolvable challenge, no doubt, because we'll never, in the end, give back as much as was given. That seems impossible, especially as the symbolic rule implies that you should give back more than is given to you. It's an arm-wrestle, then, a potlatch between the divinity and ourselves.

Is this what it means to be created in the image and likeness of God? A 'mirroring' that merely repeats this original act of God. It is perhaps a summons too, at the same time as a prohibition. There is in this, I don't mean a consolation, but . . .

Yes, there would then be a rivalry, a mimetic violence between God and man. The great game, eh! Playing God with God! With the world as the stakes. The fact remains that, if we lose at this game, if we don't manage to bring to bear an equal or greater response to meet the challenge, then we have to sacrifice this given world, to destroy it.

The fact is that, paradoxically, the equal or greater response might perhaps precisely be to sacrifice it. (Can one imagine any equal or greater response to 'creation' other than destruction?) Moreover, can one, ultimately, give it back without destroying it?

In the symbolic universe, there was a mode of sacrificial destruction: the accursed share. For one reason or another, this symbolic organization has fallen apart, and we've substituted a mode of material production and consumption for sacrifice and sacrificial consumption. This is our response, but it isn't really successful, for the sacrificial world was, admittedly, cruel, but acceptable, whereas ours is much gentler, but unacceptable. And the more consumable it is, the more unacceptable, for nothing any longer deserves to be sacrificed in it.

Or perhaps it's a still unfinished sacrifice?

Let's suppose it's an immense operation of redemption and expiation for the loss of sacrifice. This isn't the same thing at all. Is it a variant of sacrifice or the product of its excommunication? The immense process of *growth* would then be merely the manifestation of this internalized failure, the abreaction to emptiness – an unbounded work of mourning.

An immense sacrifice or an immense extermination.

It's almost impossible to decide between the two. We'd have to come back, perhaps, to the Moebius strip, to see good and evil transform themselves, as twins, into each other, since all this technical operation of the world is, more or less, the extrapolation of good, the operation of absolute good, through the obliteration of evil and the principle of evil, through the suffocation and liquidation of the accursed share. But, here again, the proliferation of good to infinity brings the parallel proliferation of its twin, absolute evil.

The Cloning of God

NOAILLES: *Yes, you even say sometimes that there's a simultaneous upsurge of good and evil. In other words, that combating evil leads to reactivating it.*

BAUDRILLARD: You've only to take the 'zero deaths' formula, a basic concept of the security order. It's clear that this equates mathematically to 'zero lives'. By warding off death at all costs (burdensome medical treatment, genetics, cloning), we're being turned, through security, into living dead. On the pretext of immortality, we're moving towards slow extermination. It's the destiny of maximum good, of absolute happiness, to lead to a zero outcome. Illusion, that is to say, evil, is vital. When you exchange this vital illusion for the unconditional promotion of Good, then you're heading for a blowback from the accursed share. This is how things are getting better and better and, at the same time, worse and worse.

But what's a mystery is that, having received a perfect duality in the beginning, we see it as our task to give back only one part of it. We don't want to give back the world in a dual mode, and the enterprise of history might be said to be a kind of attempt at annihilating one part of the duality; all in all, the conversion of the dual into the dialectical.

Human beings can't bear themselves, they can't bear their otherness, this duality; can't bear it either in the world or in themselves. They can't bear failing the world by their very existence, nor the world failing them. They've sown disorder everywhere, and in wishing to perfect the world, they end up in a sense failing themselves. Hence this self-hatred, this detestation that fuels the whole technological effort to make the world over anew. A kind of vengeance on oneself or on the human race arising out of our having contravened the order of the world by the very act of our appearance. We can't do anything about this, but it in no way diminishes the fact that the situation is unbearable. It's on this failing of existence that all religions thrive. You have to pay. In the past it was God who took the reprisals, now we do it. It's we who've undertaken to inflict the worst on ourselves, and to engineer our disappearance in an extremely complex and sophisticated way, in order to restore the world to the pure state it was in before we were in it.

Perhaps the Last Judgement has already taken place, perhaps it took place at the origin and we're carrying out the punishment.

A fine metaphysical hypothesis, except that this self-hatred is the turn taken by Western subjectivity (and also one it's currently imposing on the rest of the world). This inner verdict, this nihilism really begins only with Romanticism, but at that point it was still just an aberration. It's now become a major undertaking, an enterprise of self-immolation by technology against a background of obscure resentment at the evil spirit that's dragging us into it. So there you are: depending on how you see it, it can be taken for a challenge in suicidal form or for the enactment, as you said, of God's judgement.

What makes it look more like a punishment being carried out than a suicide is that it's taking place in slow motion.

And cloning can be said to be something like a slow-motion suicide. By that I mean not a sudden disappearance, but an innovative form of extinction of the species by scissiparity, by automatic doubling. It is, indeed, the obliteration of something by that selfsame thing – which is the definition of suicide.

This could also be a repetition of the original act, we ourselves also giving over the world to something else: in the same way as we received it, giving the world over to another species, handing on the torch. We can't do any more with it, so over to you!

It's a way of being rid of the problem, of relieving ourselves of the responsibility by devolving it to another – artificial – species; a way of telling God: 'Sort it out with them!' But that's just a dream . . . And even the future digital society, the future primitive society of the digital will have a merely uncertain existence. Without either enemy or antibodies (like the primitive cultures of the past), it'll become vulnerable once again to the slightest virus, whether electronic or biological, whether archaic or from the realms of some even more developed species. Yet one question remains: isn't the process of artificial perpetuation, if not immortality, of the species – which runs counter to evolution – itself part of evolution? (With his reversive effect and the invention of morality, Darwin himself was going against natural selection.) 'Natural' evolution wants species to disappear. It isn't just a biological fact, but a symbolic rule – doubtless the profoundest and most radical – that every species and every individual wishes both to persevere in its being, to live and survive, and at the same time to disappear. It isn't just that it's destined to disappear, but that it wants to, by another kind of will, and does all it can to do so. Human beings are opting to break that rule today, by aiming for immortality (through cloning and many other things). But aren't they actually obeying the same rule, merely deferred, or even bringing about an accelerated disappearance (there'll no longer be a human race, properly so-called, but its artificial double)? And it might perhaps be an opportunity for the human race, by putting a world of clones into orbit, to recover its original form. But God will be forced to clone himself too! It would take a clone-God to manage a world of clones.

Nietzsche's madman, who went looking for God with a lantern in the daytime, would run off horrified shouting, 'God has been cloned!' And if we've materialized the kingdom of God in this world, we've created an immanence with all the tools of transcendence, including salvation and damnation. If what Saint Thomas Aquinas cruelly points out is true ('That the saints may enjoy their beatitude and the grace of God more abundantly, they are permitted to see the punishment of the damned in hell'), it is perhaps this deep ressentiment, *this delight in the misfortune of others that's the engine of the duplication. Is it as much a question of creating an instance from which we can derive* jouissance *as of creating a species in which we can vest damnation? But what if we get the opposite outcome?*

But the real problem lies in the fact that we're already in this artificial world. Genetic clones aren't needed. We've already become clones here and now. We've already exchanged transcendence for the law of the code and of DNA. The moral law, Kant's law, the one that was written in the starry sky and in man's inner world, is now inscribed in the genetic code. There's no ideal site of consciousness any longer. And if, in the past, we could symbolically exchange this world with God under the sign of a moral law we'd invented, we can't exchange it for anything any longer, except the spectral universe that awaits us. The impossible exchange of the world is completed with the free circulation of the nothing (the exchange of the same for the same is one of the figures of the exchange of the nothing). Even in the economic field, the field of exchange *par excellence* and of value, we're beginning to realize, as generalized speculation takes over, that it's the nothing that circulates. And this is, in fact, why things are going faster and faster, no longer being hampered by either the moral law or the law of value. There's obviously an extraordinary fragility in this, which shows up in the perpetual crisis of the economic and political spheres. What we will not see is that there's much more than a crisis of operation or representation here; there is, in fact, a definitive crisis of transcendence. As we said earlier, we've moved from an upward transcendence to a downward transcendence, the last stage of which is the exchange of the nothing. But there's a complicity in this exchange of the nothing, a deep complicity that has a bright future before it because it's a collusion between criminals (and we know that that's the most solid type), between accomplices in the perfect crime. There'll no longer be anyone to say the emperor has no clothes, no longer anyone to betray the fact that all this generalized exchange is based on nothing and that it can generalize itself only on the basis of the nothing. If this were revealed, it would be the apocalypse in the literal sense, and we would stand before the nothing as a *fait accompli*.

This criminal complicity reminds me of a remark by Cioran: 'My mission is to kill time, and time's to kill me in its turn. How comfortable one is among murderers.' And the substitution of the genetic code for the moral law's a terrifying image. You can't imagine Beethoven being moved by DNA the way he was moved by Kant's dictum. The admiration of the starry sky has given way to a dread of the stars going out one by one.[11] And, reflecting on the will to accomplish the world at all costs, I think also of Borges's line: 'Aesthetics is the imminence of a revelation that is not yet produced.'[12] The originary unbearableness isn't perhaps the unbearableness of perfection but a terrible imminence that hasn't yet revealed itself and that you would have to accomplish. The world might be said to be in a state of total imminence, without ever realizing itself, without ever passing over to the other side. The temptation to complete it is too great; this imminence is the most unbearable feature of illusion and appearances. Even thought, as you've said somewhere, would be horrified at

[11] This is a clear reference to Arthur C. Clarke's story, 'The Nine Billion Names of God' (1967), to which Baudrillard has referred repeatedly in his writings.
[12] I have drawn here to some extent on Ruth L. C. Simms's translation of the relevant passage: 'that imminence of a revelation that is not yet produced is, perhaps, the aesthetic reality' (*Other Inquisitions 1937–1952* (London: Souvenir Press, 1973), p. 5).

itself and its incompleteness in its endlessly unverifiable form, and would accomplish itself as function, as desire. The chief horror would be to remain as one 'is', either a pure imminence or a total completion. The deepest horror would be to allow the word 'be' to be complicit with a static meaning. The world would abominate any form that could arrest itself in itself.

I don't recall who said that 'poetry completed what God hadn't managed to finish'.

It's only with fulfilment that there's failure. With it comes the fall into time. The lost paradise would be pure imminence, but we've always known that paradise isn't something that can be borne.

Baltazar Gracián's hypothesis is that God keeps human beings in suspense. It's his strategy to keep human beings eternally in suspense. And, for their part, human beings basically try to escape God by going to the end, by bringing about a *dénouement*.

Yes, they detest suspense. It's like in a film when you never manage to find out who did it.

And if you don't know who it was, you want to take their place.

Absolutely. You want to finish the film!

Hence this universal striving to explain the world and find the key. It always ends in the Oedipus story, where you find, obviously, that you're the criminal. The truth of the Oedipus myth isn't so much in the psychoanalytic truth about the father and the mother, but in this circular operation of revelation and detection of the crime.

Yes, when, like Oedipus, you have an extreme investigative drive – which is, in itself, a criminal attitude – the detective finds himself inside the crime a priori.

It's the signalling or beckoning of destiny we were talking about before. (In all this, God is only a metaphor). Truth, for its part, never beckons to us. It can only be the object of revelation. Only destiny beckons.

There are perhaps two moralities: you may believe in God without duplicity and in parallel with that, like Paul Virilio, carry out a radical analysis of the apocalyptic state of things.

Rather than two moralities, there might be said to be two divergent visions. The one performs an investigation that's prophetic, so to speak, describing the march towards the apocalypse in its technical twists and turns. There is, then, no secret in it: all is revealed, announced, and God himself is there, as alternative to the fateful outcome. God remains possible, and there's still a chance we may forestall the apocalypse. A prophetic, apocalyptic vision and one that's redemptive out of despair – but not a fateful vision. The fateful vision is quite different. It's that of a strategy which precipitates the world towards its end in the very effort of elucidating it and making it an ideal world. There's no longer any transcendent instance here, but the implacable unfolding of a logical process. We discover we're the criminals of this perfect crime, we're the authors of our own doom. We aren't, then, the victims of God's anger. We're within that kind of fateful irony you find in the Samarkand story, where the soldier, in order to escape death, rushes off to the place where he had an appointment with it.[13]

But isn't there a less banal, more subtle idea of God than that of belief?

Yes, in which God would be something other than an object of conviction and a final solution. In which he'd be something like the partner in a dual relationship and in which God himself would conform to the symbolic rule of exchange. But then it's no longer a question of believing in him. The question of his existence doesn't arise. Ultimately, God doesn't take himself for God and doesn't even believe in himself. At any rate, he's no longer any bigger than the game of the world [*le jeu du monde*].[14]

Being no bigger than the game of the world leads us perhaps precisely to some kind of pantheism . . . But you say that belief is the mark of a secret

---

[13] Baudrillard relates this story as follows in *Passwords* (London: Verso, 2003): 'On the town square a soldier sees death beckoning to him. He takes fright, goes to see the king and says, 'Death has beckoned to me, I am going to flee as far away as possible, I am fleeing to Samarkand.' The king commands that death be sent to him, to explain why it has terrified his captain. And death tells him, 'I didn't want to frighten him. I simply wanted to remind him we had an appointment tonight – in Samarkand.'

[14] This is the Nietzschean idea that the world deploys itself as game or play, i.e. rejecting any rule external to itself.

doubting of God. Going back to Manganelli's idea at the beginning of this dialogue, it's possible that God doesn't believe in himself precisely because he exists, and he rejects this superfluous duplication that would put him in doubt in his own eyes. Heidegger said: 'The Greeks did not believe in their gods.' Perhaps because they lived with them and dealt with them constantly.

Quite. Belief is a weak relation. It's content to worship, but it's a disintensified relation – a first step towards indifference, in fact, since it contents itself with the existence of God. Now, if God exists, there's no need to believe in him, and if you begin to believe in God, the fact is you're no longer really sure. In faith, there's no exteriority, no setting God at a distance, there's a kind . . .

. . . of immediate intensity? Do you have faith, for, as Nietzsche said, when you have it, you can afford yourself the luxury of scepticism?

Neither faith nor belief. I went from faith to belief, then to nothing. That's to say, from initially being a Christian, I became a Catholic (the person who no longer has the faith, but who still believes in it – this is the great operation of the Church, to substitute belief for faith), then agnostic. In other words, heretical in respect of all beliefs. That's all a long time ago.

And you don't have any god lingering in your bloodstream . . . ?

No god and no trace of a reality principle, because the problem has shifted today. The problem of belief has shifted from God to reality. The postulate of reality is as strong and plays the same role as belief in God did in the past. Unbelief in reality is equivalent to the agnostic heresy or the free-thinking of eighteenth-century minds. 'Those who believed in God and those who didn't . . .' – there's no longer any real friction between the two. Where the most violent demarcation line runs now, with consequences in all fields (political, moral and relational), is between those who believe in reality and those who don't (those who deconstruct its principle or have a hypothetical view of it, the 'reality perspectivists'). This denial of reality is quite simply immoral, and if there were the same intolerance as in the days when the Chevalier de la Barre was executed for not doffing his hat when a religious procession passed by, then they'd execute those who don't bow to reality today. Such agnostics and free-thinkers are rare (as were those of the eighteenth century), but, deep down, everyone (including those who believe they still believe in God) are agnostics *lite* today. Everyone toys with the disappearance of the real. We no longer believe in it deeply, and the sense that we're no longer in that line of filiation is widespread. The incontestable evidence of an objective reality has been broken down (it was a kind of mirror stage of Western rational culture), and the only consciousness we have of it is an unhappy one. But few will admit this and, if questioned, all will protest the absolute self-evidence of the real, along with their good faith, since it's as serious to deny this principle as it once was to deny the existence of God. Such a denial can emerge only from the heretical depths of a libertine consciousness.

Illusion / Real / Simulation

NOAILLES: *I'd like to talk about some key aspects of your thought. Without wishing to schematize at all or descend into facile solutions, we find a kind of triptych in your work: illusion/real/simulation. Illusion, the real as the dispelling, abstract projection and precipitate of appearances, and simulation as the ecstasy and metastasis of the real itself. This triadic pattern often recurs elsewhere in your analysis. First of all, why do you think illusion is unbearable? Why does illusion have to be dispelled by the real? Why can't we play with appearances, with forms; why do they have to be dispelled, liquidated? We could very well just take delight in this situation.*

BAUDRILLARD: Absolutely. But perhaps illusion isn't a primal scene. *Il-ludere* is to put into play, to put oneself into play. And for that you have to create the rules of the illusion.

The radical illusion of the world, as you call it, seems thinkable, at first blush, as a kind of primordial form (not in temporal terms of course).

One should be wary of this primordial, original imagining. One can imagine the world even before the appearance of human beings and thought, when there's nothing there to give it meaning, when it is, strictly speaking, without truth or reality – hence in a state of radical illusoriness. At any rate, that's what I mean by 'radical illusion', which remains the illusion today of appearances, of the pure play of appearances. But then, what does this advent of thought mean, which gives it meaning and perhaps, in a sense, hastens it towards its end? I can't yet see whether thought, as production of meaning and reduction of appearances, is what's bringing the world most rapidly to its end; ultimately, that is to say, first towards simulation, then towards disappearance. Is thought an art of disappearance?

On the one hand, I don't clearly see the location of the emergence of meaning in the appearance on the scene of human beings, who are themselves part of that emergence. Is it possible that the inclination of things towards meaning comes as much from things themselves as from the thought that brings them into play? Might meaning be conceived as another form of intersection rather than as a unilateral imposition of the subject? Is it possible that the very idea that it's thought that gives meaning is a leftover from the classical subject–object relation which is now shattered? On the other hand, it seems to me that thought can, in its extended sense, be seen as an art of disappearance. It could be the operator of the transfusion between illusion and the real, in either direction. Against the real, which is the art of making the world appear, of producing it and freezing it, thought restores the world to illusion.

It seems to me that this is the issue facing a radical thought. But there remains a mystery: what's this kind of artifice by which thought (is it the same? should we give it another name?) stubbornly persists in analysing the world, in dissolving it into simple, abstract elements and, therefore, in reducing its power of illusion?

Perhaps there might be said to be a dual, irresolvable ambivalence to thought: a thought that wishes for the absolute dis-illusioning of the world and a thought that seeks to restore the illusoriness of the world. The two forms seem to be equivalent in violence and intensity, and to have a symmetrical drive, even if they go in entirely opposite directions, and even if they don't occur simultaneously. (Radical thought does seem to respect the symbolic rule of not interacting immediately with the other form of thought, and it emerges only when analytical thought is reaching its end.) So, when thought weaves a final solution, radical thought unpicks it with equivalent or greater precision. It's even possible that the sum may, in the end, always be zero and that we've never left illusion behind! (What if the 'development' of the world were merely that rhythmic space of the exchange of illusion with itself?) In this way, thought would duplicate the radical ambivalence of the world, which never makes itself present without at the same time withdrawing, but this ambivalence would be necessary and would have a raison d'être: *it's the only way to bring the reversibility of things into play. If there were no ambivalence in thought, it couldn't possibly be reversible; if there were no ambivalence in the world, it couldn't exercise its own reversibility either. Perhaps the secret rule everything follows, including thought, is fundamentally that of setting in place this reversible movement, without final solution, which makes it possible to bring into play the* il-ludere, *the play of illusion.*

This is a really tricky question. Thought, for its part, produces the real, reality, as a challenge to illusion. What we would have, then, would no longer be illusion being debased into reality, but a duel, in which the transformation of the world under the sign of the real, squares up to the radical illusion of appearances. But thought is perhaps also merely a participant, active or passive, in appearances, of which it might be said to be a kind of subtle mirror. (A two-way mirror: appearances would be refracted in it, but on the other side of the mirror of appearances, thought could reflect [on] them without being seen.) However this may be, by dint of playing on the real and reality, thought plunges beyond objective reality, which is an unstable form, into integral reality or, in other words, into a total elimination of illusion and of the dual situation. How can illusion be sacrificed to the real? A mystery. But we may imagine that illusion takes its revenge by plunging the real into simulation, then into the virtual and into integral reality. At that stage, with the coming of artificial intelligence, the question is solved. With the virtual, the digital and information technology, the world becomes digitizable, countable, codable, absolutely real and, hence, beyond all possible illusion. All ambivalence is removed. But for that same reason, for having expelled all ambivalence, the world becomes perfectly impossible. It exists, but the fact of existing in no way detracts from its impossibility.

Having said this, we may wonder whether this digital resolution, this analytical resolution of the world might not, all the same, be a form of destiny, a destiny of disappearance by which the species might have found its final solution. Only it would be a technical solution and no longer an art of disappearing.

Yes, because disappearance isn't the same as annihilation. Now, if that were the case, just as there's an excess in operational thinking that leads the world equally into existence and into impossibility, as you say, an excess that leads the world to extermination by its artificial perfection (a perfection that transforms the world into a surplus of world), I wonder whether radical thought doesn't also, at a certain moment, cross a threshold, a form of excess greater than excess, that consigns the world back to non-existence, but perhaps also once again to possibility. (I know it's difficult to think of a supplementary form of excess on the part of radical thought, for the essence of radical thought might be said to be excess itself.) This way, in a sense, the two forms of thought would, in excess, imperceptibly exchange 'roles': it would be the destiny of operational thought to disappear, having desired for itself only a destiny of pure appearance, while radical thought would have as its destiny the recovery of a form of appearance, when it had always been its aim to disappear. (A major case of serendipity!?) Even like that, we might take the view that radical thought isn't the opposite of non-radical thought, but its dissolution, a prior state of non-scission of the two forms which contains them simultaneously, 'the violent intersection of the continuity of the world and the continuity of the nothingness', as you say, between other intersections that combine contraries before any binary scission. In this way, radical thought (ultimately, the thought of the world) could never be one of the terms of a binary opposition, but would be the seat of all duality before its conversion into something binary.

Duality and binarism are, in fact, exclusive of each other. On the one hand, duality's opposed to dialectics, in the same way as the duel is opposed to the dialogue (we are here the voluntary 'exiles from dialogue'!), but it's even more vigorously distinct from the binary and the digital. We have to distinguish clearly, in this complex game, between the dual antagonism, the dialectical opposition and the binary relation. Language itself is a source of confusion here. We must keep as clear as possible the distinction between thought (the term 'radical' adds nothing to it: if there's thought, then it's radical, come what may) and analytical intelligence (the science that Heidegger said doesn't think).

I'd like us to pose another problem: human beings themselves combine with illusion and are brought into play by it. At a certain point, a split might be said to be produced within illusion itself, and from it there emanates a 'consciousness', to put it in a provisional way, an artifice sufficiently powerful to open up a passage between two shores: the real would, in this way, be configured at a stroke, in opposition to illusion. Nietzsche pointed out that consciousness is the last and latest of the organs to evolve ('consciousness is an organ, like the stomach') and is, moreover, the most fragile in the organism. Man needs, then, a splitting into two and an immense, almost superhuman power to dis-illusion the world; and, moreover, it's with his weakest organ that he performs this feat! How can it be that part of illusion has sufficient force to dis-illusion the world? It isn't easy to conceive this collapse of the illusion through human beings; it isn't easy to conceive the possibility of wresting illusion from its own form.

Yes, our species may be said to be a kind of accelerator of disillusion. But when does this begin? Before the revolution of thought, there was the revolution of life, which is perhaps also a catastrophe. So, what lies behind our apparent course, from one catastrophe to another, from one acceleration to another, along an irreversible path towards total disillusion? In this case, the mystery is no longer in this incomprehensible process of disillusion, but in what remains that's irreducible to this movement, in what remains that's reversible and ambivalent in this apparently irreversible process.

That's right. The mystery lies perhaps as much in the world's resistance to appearing entirely in a real state as in its resistance to disappearing entirely in illusion. The world could be said to be in a kind of dynamic suspension between realization and disappearance; it would be beneath a threshold that isn't destined to be crossed in any direction.

There would, at bottom, be two ways of understanding the world: the one that considers it to be a prior given, onto which thought would graft itself – there'd be a basic reality, and everything would come down to putting together the given more or less felicitously – and the other, which thinks that the world isn't finally made, that it's a constant process of appearance, that it's in no way produced. We may, in this way, take the view that the world has never left the 'initiatory' stage. I say 'initiatory' and not 'initial' because the latter word gives the idea of a starting point for the world, from which it would be developing. The idea of the initiatory, by contrast, is a recognition of the permanent state of initiation of things, a movement that doesn't manage to yield itself up, an act that never leaves itself behind, a form of being that never transforms itself into 'has been', a world which, like a verb, couldn't and wouldn't transform itself into a participle. Clearly, we have to leave the linear hypothesis behind for all this. For the world would be there, suddenly, without ever constituting itself. Pure appearance and illusion are there; they would never take a second step, they are in a kind of pure being-outside-of-themselves (ekstatikōn), *never completing themselves. I think of Heraclitus and his famous 'Panta rhei' ('Everything flows'). It isn't a process at all, a succession; it isn't temporality at all (Heidegger said that time doesn't appear at all in Heraclitus). It would, rather, be an openness of things, an emulsion of being, but one that never manages to materialize in terms of identity.*

Yes, but I don't know whether we can imagine the world that radically, whether we can imagine a literal universe in its literalness. It can only be a great play of forms, the great play of becoming as Heraclitus saw it.

Illusion, in that sense, has no history. Illusion isn't the opposite of reality or the opposite of truth. It's a game that in no way asks itself the question of truth or reality – very Heraclitean in fact: it plays itself out, and that's all there is to it. Being initiated into that game is like being initiated into the cosmogonic play of the natural elements – water, fire, air and light – and their metamorphosis into one another. I believe the field of illusion is that of metamorphosis. We must distrust the trap of representation which makes us see illusion in a figure as static as the figure of truth. Illusion is a transfiguration.

Yes, we may tend at times to fall into the trap of stratifying illusion. Nevertheless, once we reach the point of what you call 'integral reality', that virtual and absolutely over-realized form of the world, from which all illusion is absent, I wonder whether illusion doesn't also escape towards a form of 'integral illusion', a site of absolute exclusion of the real and, in consequence, also a place that is, in a way, circumscribed and 'static'. The over-realization of the real is, ultimately, what completely interrupts the circulation of forms, and this coagulation of the world might perhaps be said to create at the same time an effect of coagulation of illusion, since illusion is such only if it sets itself in play in the world, as you were saying before. As for the term 'metamorphosis', couldn't it wrongly give the idea of a 'meta-', of a beyond?

The 'meta' of metamorphosis isn't that of metaphysics. It's a dimension of transference, of transfusion of one form into the other, without any higher instance than the game itself.

At any rate, a thing that transforms itself into another and that doesn't have its otherness within itself, so to speak, is perhaps in itself a mirage. It's difficult to conceive how otherness could be 'outside' of whatever it may be, since that 'whatever it may be' lacks identity; how could a thing have its otherness 'this side of it', since it has no limits, no inside and outside? I prefer the term 'transfiguration', because it gives the sense of a figure that never completes itself, a movement that's unceasing, yet never arrives at identity.

On condition that one understands this too as the passage from one figure to another (as in 'transcontinental') and not in the sense of 'sublimation'. As for 'otherness in itself', it seems problematical to me. I'd see, rather, an otherness outside of self, as you were saying, an otherness from elsewhere, coming precisely from beyond the subject and its identity, in the becoming of forms, and passing through neither meaning nor value. The domain of illusion is that of forms. The domain of reality is that of value. These are two opposite sides of things, perhaps two opposite destinies.

Either one starts out from reality and hypothesizes illusion, or one starts out from illusion and hypothesizes reality. Whichever way, it's a gamble. The gamble on illusion against reality, the gamble on reality against illusion. Which doubtless corresponds to a challenge: illusion's challenge to reality, reality's challenge to illusion. There's no way of getting around this. It's possible that thought produces the real not as disillusion, but as a challenge to illusion – not simply as debasement of illusion into the real or as response to unbearable illusion, but as a duel, in which the finalization or transformation of the world under the sign of the real squares up to the challenge of appearances, the challenge of a brute, literal world. We're in the area of hypotheses – the hypothesis of reality, the hypothesis of truth, the hypothesis, even, of illusion – these are all merely hypotheses. And hypotheses, by definition, aren't made to be verified. Above all, obviously, not that of illusion – to 'verify' the hypothesis of illusion would really be the end. Hypotheses are made to be pushed to their limits as hypotheses.

It's true that the expression 'otherness in itself' is very problematical. One might, in this connection, try to make a distinction. There would exist, at least, a provisional entity of things, without which nothing could come from elsewhere, and it's this entity we'd call singularity. Without this hypothesis, there'd be no forms, but unbounded chaos. It would be a singularity born within the shadow of space (which serves to prevent everything being in the same place) and within the shadow of language (which prevents everything from having the same meaning, too, as you've so aptly put it). In the singularity there's never any identity: it's delimited, but completely collapsed at the same time. (A lateral hypothesis: does multiplicity take shape only on the basis of the singular?) This singularity of forms doesn't initially presuppose an identity or a signification, so long as one doesn't force it, which realist thought will do (this will, in fact, violate Parmenides' commandment in Fragment VII: 'Never is this to be forced: that things that are not are'). Thus the singularity would not have its otherness in itself, whilst any dream of reality would bear its difference and its otherness within itself. Now, it seems to me that it isn't only the 'unbearableness' of appearances that leads to realizing them (it's perhaps a question of a duel or a challenge, as you suggest), but perhaps all things would secretly like to be outside themselves – even illusion. Would it be possible to think of a strange necessity for illusion to abandon its 'condition', even if we take the view that illusion is nothing outside the game itself? Might not the fact that it allows itself to be invested by the real be part of its very play? The real might thus be seen as a moment of the becoming of the world, as an immanent relinquishment of illusion? Can one conceive a self-challenge as an implicit movement on the part of illusion?

Being outside itself I like, and that's doubtless the most immediate figure of alterity. But for illusion to wish to be outside itself would mean it is unbearable to itself. Now, it's already in itself a form of radical otherness. How would it want to become outside itself? If we take the singularity, it doesn't strive to be outside itself, it has its own set of rules. The game itself has its rules and doesn't try to externalize all the rest, nor annex it to itself. It plays on its own account and, outside it these rules have no validity. This is the absolute horizon of appearances. As for what may be going on beyond, I know nothing of it, but there's an event internal to the illusion, to the game, to the singularity. To the work of art and the poem, if you like. Rothko was quoted, in connection with his work, as saying 'What I do opens up in all directions, but at the same time closes in all directions.' A singularity is a bit like that; something that closes up in all directions and which, at that moment, is no longer subject to any external or transcendent instance. It is to itself, as you said, its own otherness. It lives and dies that way. Primitive cultures are singularities of that order. There's a continual metamorphosis going on inside, but there's no possible transposition to other cultures.

That all things ultimately would only want to be 'outside themselves' would mean not an externalization, but that nothing would want to remain in itself, ever. Being 'outside oneself' equates to not being in oneself, while not being elsewhere either. It's like a permanent exorcism of forms and identity. Things would be eager to outflank their principle (whatever it may be), to refract themselves into another logic, to escape themselves. It's perhaps here that illusion itself diffracts itself prismatically into the real and simulation.

Well, that's something else, and the prism's a fine image. Light that diffracts itself and the spectrum of light in fact characterize the play of illusion, as it diffracts into appearances, into all the dimensions of appearance. But to go from there to saying that it diffracts into the real and simulation is something I can't conceive. The spectrality of diffraction, the spectrality of the prism or light, isn't the same thing as the spectrality of the virtual and simulation.

Yes, these are entirely different spectralities. I could try to express the idea another way: the real could be a fringe of the illusion on the inside of the Moebius strip. The instances would not be autonomizable. Doesn't the real, with its challenge, reinforce the power of illusion (beyond its provisional annihilation)? Doesn't it regenerate it with its antagonism? Doesn't illusion operate – in complete awareness of the theorem of the accursed share – by dividing itself into an antagonism beyond its radical otherness, to regenerate itself on a permanent basis? Isn't the real the zone against which illusion operates its reversibility? Could reversibility exist without a movement of the real that sought to become linear? Could seduction, for which a form of dissuasion is essential, exist without a will to production? Could it withdraw something from the order of the visible without the establishment of the visible itself? In this way, the real is perhaps what enables illusion to adopt its radical form, and the diffraction of illusion into the real would be what completes its own form. It's for this reason (though I may be completely mistaken!) that I tend to think of illusion diffracting itself and passing through the real and simulation, rather than thinking in terms of these forms being exclusive. If, going to extremes, we were to say that the coefficient of reality is proportional to the mass of illusion it displaces, we would end up with an analysis made in the substitutive light of Archimedes' Principle rather than in the reversible light of the Moebius strip. This would also pose a problem for the hypothesis of integral reality – of integral reality as compact mass that would leave all trace of illusion outside. Even if the 'provisional' autonomy of these instances is necessary for analysis.

The problem is that all this is inconceivable other than in the terms of discourse – terms which refer to one another in an endless round, a perpetual correlation – which is meaningful whether one likes it or not. This is the irremediable trap of discourse which is only ever an easy solution. Illusion is unbearable for whatever reason it may be; we have, then, to invent easy solutions, and the real is one such. As Lichtenberg said of freedom, 'It's the easiest solution and hence it is the one with the brightest future.' Only the notion of the real enables us to resist the fateful hypothesis of illusion with all that it implies of challenge, duel and death. But we always come back to the same question: Why run away from it? Why this refuge in reality as rational and objective determination?

It's rather as Nietzsche says, 'The infinite is the primordial fact, the only thing to explain would be the origin of the finite.' We know the primordial situation, but we can't locate the origin of the break.

Yes, the mystery can be said to be that of the real, of reality. And of the subject too. Why suddenly this subject effect, this subjectivity? Or again, the mystery of banality: suddenly this residue, this commonplace, statistical, random reality. In primitive organization, and doubtless in our deep mentality, chance, the 'anyhow' and the random don't exist. Everything's willed, everything's an effect of will (which clearly gives a much more exciting universe than the one ruled by causes or probabilities). It's a vision of the world, whereas the other's just a representation. Everything wants to happen, wants to become, wants to seduce – nothing's ever neutral. If we start from there, how does it come about that, at a given moment, a system of causes and effects comes to prevail? It was Nietzsche again who said, 'The effects are there, there are only effects,' adding 'with the cause as a bonus'. I find that marvellous, 'the cause as a bonus'; that what we regard as essential is something given to us 'into the bargain'! And you can go further in questioning causality (and hence, reality, since the real is what has a cause and, therefore, an objective existence) by taking up Italo Svevo's argument that 'causes are just a misunderstanding that prevents us from seeing things as they are'. What if reality itself were merely a misunderstanding? In short, we invent all that to defend ourselves against something unbearable, but something that hasn't always been so for everyone, and may exceptionally cease to be so for us too.

Causality might ultimately be said to be just a form of domestication of the idea of necessity, the conversion of this cruel aspect of the world into something digestible. The random is retrospectively inoculated to give the impression that things could possibly have not taken place. The same thing's done prospectively, and this enables us to harbour the illusion of controlling the world. The production of this commonplace reality, a colonizable reality, helps us to overcome the feeling that we're like masters without slaves in the world, though the whole drive behind it comes perhaps from the opposite, from the feeling that we're slaves without masters! Moreover, it's much easier to sacrifice a banal universe, as virtual reality will do with the real, after having sacrificed the symbolic universe. It's a minor crime after a major one, like looting after warfare. Now, if the 'unbearable' hasn't always been so for everyone, it becomes difficult to identify the moment at which – and the reason why – a species sees itself suddenly terrorized by its symbolic universe, the moment at which it feels compelled to replace vision by representation (can we conceive that it's the fatal attraction of illusion, the fear of collapsing into it once and for all, the terrifying homologation with it, that leads us constantly to murder it and develop a will for its opposite?) Though we may wonder whether the 'bearability' of illusion among primitives isn't a kind of opposite projection that would be re-creating a lost paradise.

Of course we can always dream, and no one will ever be able to prove it. But it's in theoretical terms that this is interesting. And we can guess at it analogically, through language, which remains a living utopia and a much more proximate singularity. You can see that the singularity of language has never disappeared. Even instrumentalized as a means of communication, there's a hard core of literalness in language that seems to me irreducible. Signification is only the part of language that shows above the surface. In its form and sequencing, it still retains the singular potency which means, indeed, that one language isn't comparable with any other.

Gradation / Degradation / Hierarchy

NOAILLES: *So should we think of the instances of illusion, real and simulation as a gradation? Is there a transition from one to the other? That seems difficult to me.*

BAUDRILLARD: There would, rather, be a degradation.

But that's more or less the same thing, the same story in reverse, the story of an impoverishment of appearances, of a shrinkage of illusion. I can only imagine the real and illusion coexisting, without either of them being the starting point, without the pre-eminence of the form of illusion (which poses the problem of the origin of the real). Ultimately, one couldn't privilege either of the terms of the challenge. That's why I feel attracted by the prismatic idea rather than by the idea of gradation/degradation. If there's a gradation, then we've two problems: the movement and the hierarchy between the instances.

The schema of gradation – or degradation – would be like this: a radical initial (initiatory) form, that of illusion – the real is the extenuated, disintensified form of this – and an even more disintensified simulation, the minimal phase. On the fringes of the virtual and the hyperreal (the extreme phase of simulation), we're as far as possible from illusion and seduction; we're in what I call integral reality, the end-point of that vertiginous undertaking of the realization of the world. At the height of simulation – in other words, at the height of the virtual and the digital – we're in the pure operation of a world expurgated of any illusion, and hence perfectly real, technically realized. All this, which seems in fact to constitute a single, linear, graduated or degraded, apparently irreversible process – an almost entropic process – can be seen as more or less the opposite of Hegel's ascent towards Absolute Spirit.

But this isn't the last word on the subject, since this single, irreversible process is, in fact, shot through with, and undercut from within by, duality and reversibility, in which is condensed the power of illusion as form, not as original ideal stage (as the reference to primitive societies may unfortunately imply, with its suggestion of illusion as lost object). If you bring this rule of reversibility into play, then at the height of obscenity, you find seduction again. Or Heidegger saying that, at the extreme limit of technology, you rediscover the 'constellation of the mystery'.[15] And this reversion doesn't just come at the end, in the terminal phase. This oppositionality develops and grows in parallel throughout the process, in a latent or varyingly violent form. At the heart of reality itself, something like illusion re-emerges – and this certainly isn't dialectical; it's the decisive stakes of a dual, antagonistic form.

That's an extremely interesting point. First, I think that if we were dealing with the inversion of the Hegelian movement, we'd perhaps run the risk of

[15] 'La constellation du secret'. The standard French translation by André Préau reads: 'la constellation, le mouvement stellaire du secret' ('La question de la technique', in *Essais et conférences* (Paris: Gallimard, 1958) p. 45). William Lovitt renders the German as 'the constellation, the stellar course of the mystery' (*The Question Concerning Technology and Other Essays* (New York: Harper & Row, 1977), p. 33).

being forced to apply to any idea of regression the same arguments as we've used to criticize metaphysically the idea of progress (or progression). What's difficult for me to conceive is just this coexistence of the idea of progression / regression with that of reversibility, locating the reversibility at the end of the process, 'after the orgy'. Starting from there, it seems to me that history could be the 'micro' development of what happens with Being on a 'macro' scale. The being 'outside of itself' of that which exists, the 'there is' [il y a], seems to develop as an irreversible process. And this is perhaps merely deceptive, in the same way that history, which seems to be consolidating itself as process, is in reality, as you say, being undermined from within by its reversible form. No linear form manages to constitute itself, even though it seems to make great headway. The same thing might be seen as taking place at the level of the initiatory movement of the world: no consolidation of an identity, no conversion of one thing into 'something else' can take place because there's a permanent reversibility that undermines any emergence (apparition). It's the powerful dynamics of emergence, which dissolves any possibility of identity at the very outset. I'm aware, however, that this raises an almost insoluble problem: it's a vision that leads to a universe that's so dynamic it's almost static. It's a form of absolute velocity, a way the world has of being rapid without moving. To this is added the difficulty that one can scarcely account for the externalization of movement. But Zeno brings relief on this point! (Borges described Zeno brilliantly as the 'denier that anything can happen in the universe', which I find particularly alluring.)

 This is perhaps what happens when thought leaves 'Euclidean' space behind. We may think of what McLuhan is indicating in his Global Village: *in the scene in* Star Wars *at the precise moment when Han Solo sets his spacecraft to a particular speed, all the points of light remain static. By travelling faster than light, the spacecraft becomes simultaneous, and it's everywhere at once. (What McLuhan described as a property of acoustic space, by opposition to the Euclidean and the visual, is a space whose centre is everywhere.) But, suggestively, McLuhan said of that space (a retrospective echo of your own thought?) that it's 'a proper place for the birth of metamorphosis'.*

As a methodological strategy, it may perhaps be necessary to posit the hypotheses of the real, simulation and integral reality for a theoretical development to be possible, since, if we merely accepted the hypothesis of illusion, that development would be cancelled out too soon (it would seem necessary also to avoid the silence or ineffable expression we would arrive at by that route), since the hypothesis that everything is reversible simultaneously in the very act of emergence runs the risk of being an excessively rapid return to the starting point, the risk of never getting beyond that starting point . . . Yet the hypothesis of illusion, the real and simulation also enables us to hypothesize linearity, that Euclidean form of thought. Perhaps everything in the universe is working towards a return to illusion. Perhaps that's its sole mission, and integral reality would be a perverse short-cut which, as you say, opens up a space for 'a thinking freed from all purpose, all "objectivity" and restored to its radical uselessness',[16] the poetic 'transference of situation'. The mother of all reversibilities! The hyperbolic form acquired by the world would be led inevitably to send itself back to its starting point.

Lastly, what you say about the re-emergence of seduction at the high point of obscenity is true only of someone who's thoroughly grasped the rule of reversibility. In this sense, it's a tricky expression, a paradox and a danger too, since one could make this concession only after having made a radical critique, as you've done.

We must, in fact, steer clear of the assumption of an original illusion. Illusion isn't nostalgic, it's immanent, it's an immanent reversion. It must

---

[16] Jean Baudrillard, *Impossible Exchange* (London: Verso, 2001), p. 111.

emerge not from an ideal alternative, but from the state of things as it is. It's almost impossible to perform a radical phenomenology of illusion without bringing in assumptions from elsewhere. Yet, it's in this way, by a spectral analysis, so to speak (in the likeness of this spectral reality of simulation and of the technical identification of the world), that you may try to find – not re-find – or invent the form of illusion, almost as though it had never existed; that you may try to produce it out of the very internal failing of the operational system. Beyond a critical analysis of simulation itself, ultimately caught in the trap of simulation, one has to see through to reality as an untenable paradox, with its hiatuses, slips and antibodies – something that's coming apart at every moment. It's this one must see through to – whether we call it illusion or not – this irreducible antagonistic power. Illusion has no existence in itself; it's reality that produces it, like a kind of magnetic field. In this sense, reality does, indeed, outstrip fiction and all the critical analysis you can perform on it.

The fact that illusion isn't an ideal alternative, but emerges out of a state of things, reminds me of your distinction between evil [mal] and misfortune [malheur]: 'Evil is the world as it is, misfortune is the world as it should have been.' I'm happy illusion isn't doomed to an unhappy [malheureux] destiny! Now, if all precedence of illusion over the real or of the real over illusion is impossible, the two phenomena will become inseparable, despite their antagonism and their irreducibility. To dream of a precedence is possible only within the mirage of linearity, in the conformation of which radical analysis itself doubtless plays a role, for we're necessarily obliged to carry out such an analysis in a linear fashion, as we were saying earlier, even if we incorporate the convulsions as we go along or if we do it in a language homologous to the language of illusion, retaining the paradoxical form. Even if we can try to speak of the world as Apollinaire did in his Calligrammes: *to speak of a horse he traced its outline with the poem; to speak of rain he had it fall in lines . . .*

Discourse is, in fact, discursive by definition. In other words, it's linear and non-reversible. But without going so far as the poetic mode, you can subsume the philosophical paradox in a kind of spiral. Consciousness analyses the world, but itself forms part of the world, and hence its claim to analyse it is itself part of the very operation of the world. Thought is, therefore, by homology, part of the general illusion by virtue of this enfolding, this embedding, of the one in the other. However far you go in objective analysis, you still remain in an operation that's itself part of appearances: that is to say, an operation that has no basis of any kind in a consciousness external to the world. This is where the secret lies, in this involuntary complicity, of a true – and I would even say poetic – grasp of the phenomenon of the world. The world, said Wittgenstein, is what is the case. And consciousness is the case too, of course. But it can't claim any kind of privilege. It's there, so to speak, as a bonus (as Nietzsche said about causes in relation to effects). It's the world that affords itself the luxury of consciousness.

Yes, this paradox of consciousness, as integral part of the world, analysing the world, is also given form in Nietzsche's words: 'An instrument of knowledge that wants to know itself. The stomach that digests itself.' And Wittgenstein too had this fine image: the difficulty thought finds itself in is like the difficulty of someone who's in a room and would like to leave it. First he tries the window, then the fireplace, but to no avail, and he would only have to turn round to see that the door has been open all along! You can't, in fact, imagine a stronger force than illusion. You could only instantiate the real by a kind of ruse of illusion itself. If you think of the impoverishment in this transition between illusion, the real and simulation, you invert the hierarchy, but leave hierarchy itself in place. Nietzsche again said that the pathos of distance, the sense of hierarchical distance, lies at the deepest heart of any morality. Perhaps we have before us an ultra-sophisticated form of morality, its non-Euclidean form, for what seems difficult to me is to escape from the trap of foundation, once one overturns the hierarchy.

To escape that, to escape the phantasm of evolution or of an original reference, I can see only one solution. Each phase of this process (which is not, in fact, a process) has to have its perfection in itself; it has to be taken in its absolute singularity, without any possible comparison and, hence, without hierarchy. The flower is as perfect as the fruit. Childhood has its singularity, and old age too. Nothing culminates at a universal destination – not even the human species. According to Nietzsche, it isn't true that the ideal of the human race lies in its highest happiness. We can envisage something much better: a specific happiness or misfortune, a personal destiny and not a general destination. Any race, species, age or sex has its secret rule. 'Each cloud has its own repose,' says Hölderlin. Instead of that, we constantly have one eye on generality, and that's when the regime of differences and discriminations sets in. Lichtenberg thought we were dead before we were alive – in other words, there was already a specific state before life. In seeing things that way, he broke down the evolutionary curve of life, which would mean going from life to death. Death is there first, life afterwards. It's like saying: illusion, nothingness is there first; something, the real is there afterwards. But there's neither priority nor privilege in this. Each state is an exceptional one. And what thought must do, if it can, is to except each fragment from the whole to retain its specific character.

GRADATION / DEGRADATION / HIERARCHY

That idea of perfection is, to some extent, the opposite of what Cioran said: 'Theology and metaphysics abdicate before the authority of the trivial detail.' I prefer your idea that in the detail each thing is perfect, and that, taken overall, the world is decidedly disappointing. We could at least agree that, whether it's in the detail or in the whole, perfection's never in both at once! And I also like the idea of a perfection immanent in each singularity (one knows that this is difficult, nevertheless, for if it were the case, we'd be obliged to conceive a perfection of the real, of simulation, of integral reality, etc., and it seems that critical energy could find itself for some moments bereft of its fuel, which is denunciation). But, at the same time, this doesn't prevent the idea that each phase has its own perfection being a very fine one. Perhaps we cannot really choose between the hierarchy or the perfection of the world? (Perhaps the world is dynamically hierarchical and statically perfect?)

These are thoughts akin to Zen, as we were saying before. The Zen pronouncement about mountains and rivers doesn't make any comparisons, even though it seems difficult not to understand it as a process (is it possible to conceive a process without either evolution or involution?). The third stage is just like the first, literally, but it isn't the same at all. You say, 'It is as though we had passed from a universe that does not yet know value or the sign function to a universe of sign value, commodities and meaning, and then again – but this is not the same at all – to a universe that no longer knows value and which is, then, the site of a total, undifferentiated equivalence.' When you cast off transcendent difference, that doesn't mean at all that you enter into indifference. There's a kind of new immanent difference. Might the world itself be organized not around a transcendence or an order of values, but rather in an immanent fashion, in terms of its nearness to, or distance from, illusion?

An immanent attraction, yes, as in a magnetic field. And, over against that, an immense process of deregulation.

But to distinguish between its stages, 'hierarchy' seems to slip unavoidably into the analysis. It's a little bit like in the extremes of seduction and simulation: simulation also abolishes the real, as does seduction, but between the two there's a difference of enchantment.

Yes, a considerable difference. They have in common this oblivion, this obliteration of meaning, but that's a negative common denominator. The liquidation of meaning in the virtual is merely the zero degree of meaning, the 'this side' of signification. Whereas seduction is a 'beyond' of meaning, by resolution and absolution. From the standpoint from which you were talking, it's the stage after the learning of Zen: a form that could be said not even to have the idea of meaning and to function without even the hypothesis of meaning. But it sometimes seems difficult, from just this point of view of meaning, to differentiate between the extremes. It's the same with impossible exchange. We have here two incomparable opposite figures: on the one hand, impossible exchange by default, the type that affects our system of generalized exchange, which ultimately turns out to be impracticable, and, on the other, impossible exchange from excess, that of inexchangeable singularities. Impossible exchange, then, on either side of a zone of conventional exchange.

Yes, the difficulty is that we're prisoners of the perspective of meaning, the true motive force behind the desire to resolve this problem. In this connection, Jean Cohen distinguished three instances: conventional language, absurd language and poetic language. Conventional language has denotation, but no connotation; absurd language shatters conventional language and has neither denotation nor connotation; poetic language has no denotation, but it does have connotation. In other words, the two – the absurd and the poetic – have shattered conventional language. I'm tempted to establish a correspondence between these three orders of language and the orders of illusion, the real and simulation. The order of illusion would be that of the poetic, a kind of 'primordial' language, a non-reductive form of the world. Conventional language would be a violation of that language, in the way that the real violates illusion (in my opinion, it isn't at all poetic language that shatters conventional language, but the opposite). The real would thus be the equivalent of conventional language, and perhaps simulation would be comparable to the instance of the absurd, even though simulation is not absurd at all – that universe which lies this side of connotation and also of denotation, the absurd as pure and simple predator on meaning, which uses the same weapons as meaning to liquidate it, a form of rupture which remains nonetheless indebted to meaning, a form of disintegration of the sign and the impossibility of finding an equivalent for it.

Poetic language has no meaning, but, nonetheless, it isn't the language of the absurd and of meaninglessness. A large part of modern art and poetry, including Surrealist art and poetry, has invented a whole sphere of meaninglessness and absurdity. That's all part of the destruction of meaning, but it's merely the broken mirror of meaning. It isn't a singular poetic form which, for its part, has no concern for meaning or meaninglessness.

Finalistic language is the static photograph of a world that's always elsewhere. The real and the conventional are merely a condensation at a point, a truce language affords itself so as to be able to appear. One might say that, in the poetic, negativity is given as added extra, never as a condition of the poetic. The poetic creates the rupture because it is; *it isn't the rupture that brings it into being. It's rather like what Roland Barthes says about Japan: 'The haiku's task is to achieve exemption from meaning within a perfectly readerly discourse (a contradiction denied to Western art, which can contest meaning only by rendering its discourse incomprehensible).'[17] This is what distinguishes illusion, and what you call signalling, when something signals in an untranslatable, yet intelligible way. In* Fatal Strategies, *you say, 'It is not enough for a story to be illogical and senseless to be seductive, it also has to signal enigmatically.'[18] In illusion and seduction, something signals, and this does not occur in simulation. What might this signalling be – the signalling or beckoning, for example, in the story of death in Samarkand? What distinguishes this signalling, beyond its addressee, from any other act in the world?*

This isn't the sign in the semiological sense of the term. It's the *Witz*, the shaft of wit or the allusive wink. It isn't about communication, but about an immediate secret complicity. It's an allusion, and in that regard akin to illusion, without lexicon or syntax; it's elliptical and always of the order of seduction,

[17] Roland Barthes, *Empire of Signs*, trans. Richard Howard (New York: Hill & Wang, 1983), p. 81.
[18] I have stayed with Valiente Noailles's version of this passage here, though he is clearly either quoting from memory or retranslating the Spanish translation when he says: 'Il ne suffit pas qu'une histoire soit illogique et insensée pour être séduisante, il faut encore qu'elle *fasse signe* de façon énigmatique' (*Les Exilés du dialogue*, p. 83). In *Les Stratégies fatales*, Baudrillard actually writes not 'de façon énigmatique', but 'de façon inintelligible', which seems rather more radical. For some reason, the English translation of *Les Stratégies fatales* by Beitchman and Niesluchowski adds a further complication by rendering the second clause as 'it is still necessary *that this be signalled* in an unintelligible way' (*Fatal Strategies* (New York: Semiotext[e]/Pluto, 1990), p. 136).

as though coming from elsewhere and, most of the time, as in the Samarkand story, it's linked to a fateful occurrence. We might say, then, that there are three stages (again!): that of the trace or *trait*; that of the sign properly so-called; and, in the current state of the digital, that of the cipher [*chiffre*], in which there's no longer any trace of a sign.

This triptych form seems unavoidable in analysis: metamorphosis/metaphor/ metastasis, antagonism/Aufhebung/Steigerung, otherness/difference/indiffer- ence, dual/polar/digital, etc.

Yes, but the fundamental argument remains that of duality. The triptych mustn't lead us to forget that, ultimately, everything is played out in a quasi-Manichaean clash in which the shadow of the principle of evil can be seen to loom – unless the forces grappling with each other aren't doing so frontally and the principle of evil in this case takes the form of reversibility. Analysis may distinguish moments in a process, the finality of which we don't perceive (it runs off into an indeterminate dimension), but that doesn't render the antagonistic postulate invalid, the fact of two powers exclusive of each other and irreconcilable. Between illusion and integral reality, between seduction and production, between radical otherness and the systematic identification of the world, there's no possible compromise; the confront- ation between them is irresolvable. The only relation can be one of reversion (neither inversion nor subversion, but reversion). The analytical order is something conceived by the mind, it's the mind working. But reversibility isn't something played out by the subject, it's the working of the world itself. This rule of the overall game – duality and reversibility – is to a large extent beyond our grasp. But many metaphysics have envisaged it. It isn't perhaps very far from the myth of Eternal Return. But we can barely represent this to ourselves in space or in mental space. It's difficult to give it material form in some dimension or other. Some theories in physics come close: that of the double arrow of time, for example, with the hypothesis of the Big Bang and the Big Crunch beginning simultaneously. But we're sliding towards science fiction a bit there.

I can see this primacy of the dual over the triptych-style analysis. Let's think about these other 'couples' of terms: immanence / transcendence, surface abysses / depth, secret / decipherment, reversibility / linearity, rule / law, observance / belief, pataphysics / metaphysics, rituality / sociality, etc. There's no frontal relation: the first term of the pair isn't linked dialectically to the second. It functions rather as a solvent of the irreversible pretensions of the second. The first term is anterior to the slash between the two, anterior to the distinction that instantiates the real between the two. Ultimately, perhaps, everything would be readable as duality and as triptych. The first seems to be a state of things preliminary to the instantiation of any binary divide; the second is a concept that emerges naturally from that divide. Perhaps the fundamental difference between these two analytical matrices plays out in a secret tone of reconciliation or irreconciliation. Isn't the triptych-style analysis imperceptibly orientated towards a form of resolution, a temptation to synthesis that would put an end to the antagonism? Doesn't the third axis of the triptych operate at times as a deus ex machina *attempting to resolve conceptually that which is irresolvable? Every duality that begins to be understood in a binary fashion necessarily calls forth a third element (the dialectic is always fertile, even if it eventually summons up cloning!), whereas a duality understood as such has no need to eliminate duality. In this Manichaean duel, we might wager that seduction would become more powerful than production, because it has become syntonic with the reversible modality of the world. So far as the other term is concerned, reversibility comes to it* de facto, *it isn't incorporated into its form; on the contrary, indeed, it dispels reversibility. And, to return to our original triad, it seems there's one term too many. I wonder what the density of the real might be today, between illusion and simulation.*

Very low. What's the credibility of the real today? This brings us back to some degree to our initial proposition, that of God's atheism. If reality's no longer dependable, that's because it has no confidence in itself any longer. It's become confused with banality and with the fall into banality. But there are, paradoxically, two points it comes down at: radical illusion and integral reality (the virtual). In other words, it falls either by relinquishment of its own principle or by exceeding its own principle. In the meantime, it constitutes a rallying point by default, a collective convention, so to speak – a kind of compulsory club, whose outdated ceremonial one accepts. Groucho Marx said, 'I wouldn't join a club that would have me as a member.' Well, reality is the virtual club we're co-opted into in spite of ourselves (and, like Groucho, we don't necessarily want to be members). In fact, there no longer are any members, but it serves nonetheless as a referent and a moral code. If you reject it, anathema ensues. Immorality has now come to refer entirely to the denial of reality, to the questioning of reality. The taboo of reality has replaced the sexual taboo. And that taboo is so strong only because reality is currently disappearing.

Yes, the real might be said to be a form of purgatory for the original crime, but a purgatory which, paradoxically, we find quite comfortable because it defers the decision on where we come down. Despair increases as the real's room for manoeuvre shrinks because the alternative you speak of then becomes inevitable: coming down in illusion or, ultimately, in integral reality. The more the real disappears, the more there's panic. And, to fuel its existence,

71

the real demands sacrifices to its gods: and, naturally, they start with the heretics who speak against it.

And even more, what speaks to one side of it, outside its field, and no longer takes it into account. But realist thought takes its revenge. It confuses the messenger with the 'bad' news (that of the death throes of the real). It sees a conspiracy in this and makes you the objective accomplice of those things you are trying to read against the grain. It confuses you with Le Pen, for example, or terrorism, if you venture to speak 'dangerously' about them. All irony, all distance has disappeared from the intellectual field. The cult of the real, of the lost object, dominates us with all its bad conscience.

Yes, in the eyes of realist thought, everything is functional: by the very fact of exploring the scene of the crime, radical thought lays itself open to being charged with the murder. The strategy consists in deflecting exploration from another hypothesis: that of an assisted suicide of the real, a suicide from an incapacity to tolerate the overload of meaning. Responsibility must be assigned to someone in the hope that, if ironic discourse is eliminated, the problem itself will be also.

Realism is a magical thinking. Like magical thinking, it takes words for things. Integral reality interprets everything, the negative and the positive, in the same sense and by the same value criterion, that of a total positivity. No negativity any longer, no critical thought – that's the price to pay for joining the club. Now, even if we were able to analyse the 'critical illusion', we did so in the sense of a radical thinking, of a 'beyond' of critical thinking. Here, we're up against a liquidation, a reduction and immediate digestion of anything that can constitute opposition. It's like a form of virus that devours immunities and leaves us defenceless. 'Objective' reality was always in some way a critical reality: it carried out its own defence. In the face of extreme reality we are, by contrast, defenceless. We cannot but feel nostalgic, then, for that critical spirit produced by the Enlightenment, which appears, retrospectively, as a historical singularity – when faced with an integrist real which, having to some degree eliminated the rational, has retained conceptual energy only so as to exterminate what remains of it.

It's terrifying, this kind of nuclear winter that's spreading over theory and the world, which eliminates at birth the slightest trace of life. If, out of panic, illusion has been eliminated, the traces of illusion must also be wiped out. We're confronted with the pluperfect crime.

Yes, all illusion must be hounded out, particularly the sacrificial forms. I'm thinking of the Spaniards landing in Mexico, who could very well have exploited the gold and the Indians without exterminating them. Yet they had a major reason for doing so. The fact was that the Spaniards had already, at that time, lost the sense of the sacred; they'd already ceased to invest in their religious faith, and they quite simply couldn't tolerate a people that went as far as human sacrifice in its religious ritual. Such striking proof of an intense faith arouses fierce jealousy among those who've lost it. This example encapsulates the entire modern enterprise of an undifferentiated world, our world, which cannot but exterminate any kind of singularity or difference.

Why is singularity experienced as a threat? It's a mystery similar to that of the logic that leads us to exterminate illusion: the act of extermination occurs

73

repeatedly against anything which, like illusion, shows a spark of difference and intensity. Although, without doubt, the hypothesis of a fierce jealousy is also the reason for the violence exerted against any form of singularity, against any area attesting to an ironic reserve on the part of the world? However, the duel is lethal and hopeless for realist thought: whilst its enemy grows in its entrails, it dreams of conquering it by annihilating it from the outside.

In our world, the only good singularity is a dead one. Or – but this is the same thing – a singularity resuscitated and locked away in our museum universe. The exterminated Indians are being given a territory again today and a social existence. The bodies of their ancestors are being returned to them, and they're even being turned into casino managers. That's the Disneyland operation, in which all that's disappeared is artificially restored. But all modern nations have built themselves up – and continue to do so – on the basis of an extinction of local singularities or their assimilation into folklore. And what will there be at the end of this total absorption? In the heart of this indifference, unfortunately, there's still enough nostalgia and remorse to carry the extermination through to the end. That nostalgia, which takes the form of humanitarian redemption and remorseless protection, is, in fact, the best way of finishing the job. We're the only culture that's ever committed itself to an undertaking of this kind. The others could be violent and conquering, but they didn't aim for this annihilation, this global moronization.

This lobotomization is even worse than violence.

Yes, because violence is still a dual relation, an antagonistic relation, whereas there's a form of pure elimination here, of mental genocide. It's what you see, too, in the recent 'wars' (which, for that very reason, weren't wars): the extermination of the enemy as enemy, their disqualification as opponents. They don't exist, their character of enemy is wrested from them, the very possibility they might have of fighting. I don't remember who it was who said that war means destroying the other side's quality of light. What has happened in Afghanistan? The disqualification of that country and the installation of the global order (including in the form of music, television, democracy and tearing off the veil). But, beyond the strategic and political conflict, all wars ultimately have this objective and this main effect: the destruction of singular cultures and of everything that resists the global order and generalized exchange. Anthropological genocide.

Transcendence / Immanence

BAUDRILLARD: Not only the stage of the real, but that of the sign itself is behind us today and has been absorbed into the virtual and the digital. This marks, as it were, the decline of simulation and of the theory of simulation, of what will very soon seem to us to have been a golden age of the simulacrum. In simulation, the real is to a great extent set at a distance, but there's still the shadow of a lost signification, an underlying vision of the real. Simulation has run out of signs, but it hasn't really broken with the classical analysis of representation. It's still an interplay between two similar qualities, between reality and virtual reality.[19] When the virtual wins out, this

---

[19] The French here is 'entre chien et loup', which is to say between two things that are difficult to distinguish. The expression is commonly used in French to indicate nightfall, the point at which one cannot distinguish between dog and wolf. As such, it can apparently be traced back at least to a Hebrew text of the second century BC.

complex game of the sign and its substitution for the real comes to an end. The dialectic of meaning and the equilibrium of the sign first give way to the disequilibrium of meaning and signification in the simulacrum (there's no longer any general equivalent in the real, the sign can no longer be exchanged for reality), then, at the highest stage of simulation, to the fractalization of meaning in the digital, to acceleration into the void. One no longer even has that alienation of meaning that still corresponded to the notion – and the society – of the spectacle. There's no longer even the shadow of a reference. Figures and digital calculation (the 0/1 which is no longer a difference at all, but a formal alternation) lay hold of information and of the whole sphere of artificial intelligence. The differential calculus of the sign gives way to the integral calculus of the virtual. There's been much talk of the murder of reality by the sign, but that hypothesis needs to be nuanced: more serious than the murder of the real is the murder of the sign. And if the phase of simulation is indeed that of the murder of the real, the virtual, for its part, is the phase of the murder of the sign.

NOAILLES: *It's the move from a parody of the real to the real without any parody. It's fantastic to see how the Zen 'progression' comes into play again, although still inverted: from the universe that knows no value to the universe of value and the sign, then 'once again' to a universe that no longer knows any value. Might we be moving from a shadow that distantly evoked a body to a body that succeeds, by way of revenge, in ridding itself entirely of its shadow? The simulacrum still conformed, perhaps, to the last degree of the inversion of Platonism. But in this additional step, in the death of the sign, the world goes further, towards the recognition not only that there aren't two worlds, but that there isn't even one. A world that eliminates its shadow, its phantasmatic form, is the most concrete form of impossibility. But I greatly like this image you use: by doing away with transcendence, we've materialized the kingdom of God immanently. The total realization of transcendence in immanence.*

In Saul Bellow, there's this idea that transcendence is still there, but it's downward transcendence now, not upward.

That's lovely, a bit like Hölderlin's image of falling upwards. In Saul Bellow, so to speak, it's transcendence towards the before rather than the beyond. Ultimately, there's a kind of drive towards transcendence that we can't do without. As for immanence, there's the rather Spinozan idea of an absolute coextensiveness of the real and the possible, a perfect coextensiveness, entirely opposite to Leibniz's theory of one world among other possible worlds. In the same way as, for Spinoza, what is in potentia in God exists necessarily, and what doesn't exist, necessarily isn't possible. (If something were possible but didn't exist, God wouldn't be all he could be; he wouldn't be infinite.) You might say that it's the dialectical negation of the world that opens up 'the possible' as alternative and that pure affirmation, for its part, closes the field of the possible. To conceive the necessity of the world and not its random character immediately rules out any space beyond. Hegel himself defined necessity in the Encyclopaedia of the Philosophical Sciences *as 'the union of possibility and actuality'.[20] It would seem that the world conceived as impossible exchange, without equivalent beyond or before it, can only be such if it's conceived as completely necessary.*

[20] The English reader may be more familiar with a reference here to Hegel's *Logic*. The precise reference is: *Hegel's Logic. Being Part One of The Encyclopaedia of the Philosophical Sciences (1830)*, trans. William Wallace, with a Foreword by J. N. Findlay (Oxford: Clarendon Press, 1975), §147, p. 208.

In the past, the virtual had the possibility of becoming actual [*réel*]. Actuality was even its destination. There was, then, possibility. Today, when the virtual is winning out over the real, there's no longer any possibility, since everything is immediately realized. We have, then, here again, if you like, an absolute coextensiveness, though not, as in Spinoza, by ideal adequation, but rather, by confusion and mutual cancelling. In the virtual, there's no longer any actual, since any other actual is simultaneously possible; there's no longer any possible, since all the possibilities are immediately realized. The result is acceleration into the void . . . the desert, as I put it. The Real is the desert, and the Real is growing like the desert. 'Welcome to the desert of the real,' as they say in *Matrix*, that perfect illustration of virtual reality. The metaphysical immanence of Spinoza has given way to the operational immanence of the virtual.

Once arrived at the point of a pure operational immanence, without distance, transcendence or signification, then we may wonder whether illusion might ultimately be destructible.

I'm torn between the idea of an integral calculus of the world, and hence of a definitive loss of illusion, and that of an indestructible form of illusion. Not by a privileging of the origin, for if illusion were originary, it could come to an end, but by a kind of fatal strategy internal to the system itself, which ensures the reintroduction of something indestructible that thwarts it – something one may call illusion, but one of the forms of which may quite simply be thought [*la pensée*].

For what does the immense episode of materialization, doubled by artificial intelligence, ultimately give way to, once it has reached its perfection or, in other words, once the perfect crime has been perpetrated? It gives way to thought: to thought, the sole master of the void, as ascendancy of the void and ascendancy over the void, into which ultimately this integrally realized world plunges itself. Physics offers us a metaphor for this void; it's no longer the void in which there's nothing, but a void charged with potentiality, a potential void, and thought would be this potential of the void. If we push these lines of thinking as far as we can, the extremes surely meet, the desert of the virtual and the potential void of thought meet – like that stucco angel, the allegory of the virtual, whose extremities meet in a curved mirror. These are all 'fatal' hypotheses.

The Vaccinated System

NOAILLES: *To think politics a little and to come back to Europe, I'd like us to talk about the strange rise of the extreme Right and the disappearance of the Left.*

BAUDRILLARD: The Left has long been living a merely phantom existence; it's a long time since it had a political will of its own. The same goes for the Right, by the way: they're both disappearing together. In fact, it's the distinction between them that's disappeared and with it the stakes on the political scene. That's why the only political discourse today is that of Le Pen who, for his part at least, articulates this objective complicity, this confusion, between Right and Left. That is, in a sense, the basic truth which the entire activity of the political class strives to mask. But since, ultimately, the Right is part of normal life and the everyday scenery, it's the Left, as emblem of the political, that will be mourned.

Perhaps we're still in the evil / misfortune [mal/malheur] *difference here, since the Left to some extent represents the world as it should have been.*

Yes, and so it embodies misfortune. In a sense, that's entirely to its credit. As the vehicle of the social ideal (not to speak of revolution), it's dying from the death throes of the social itself. It's a long time since anyone thought of the Right as having a social agenda; it might be said, rather, to be the 'degree zero' of politics, and it remains in being as such because it's the easiest solution. The Left itself, which was the marked term, is no longer either marked or remarkable. But, all the same, it still takes itself for the divine Left. It can scarcely claim any historic privilege any more, but it still claims to retain a moral privilege.

The idea that it's still the vehicle and repository of meaning.

Yes, but for there to be meaning, there has to be difference. When general equivalence sets in, the confrontation between Left and Right is no longer anything but a closed, zero-sum exchange. Instead of giving a political form to their action, they merely exchange themselves for each other in a fictive alternation. And, as a result, it's the political that becomes impossible to exchange. This is what has been pointed up by Le Pen, who, in his very ubuesque emergence, embodies that impossibility. By stigmatizing this equivalence, he appears as the only marked term; all the others are the degree zero. He's the evil, the one who speaks and bears evil, and the fact he's a grotesque individual is of no importance – that's the irony of evil. He's the evil [*le mal*], and the others are in misfortune [*le malheur*]. They manage the perpetual misfortune, for want of confronting the evil. This situation is irresolvable, since the idea of putting evil in power makes no sense either. The point is to do evil to power, not to put evil in power.

And perhaps he'd turn into an absolute moderate . . .

He'd become part of the political game, that's certain. Evil can irrupt, but it isn't made to last. It can only be an exception. Many in the political class have sensed this creeping evil, and they've tried to find a homeopathic solution for it, letting a little dose of doubt, confession, irony and contestation seep in – the devil's share – but, of course, they can't pull it off, despite this 'ill' will, since the system is vaccinated – self-vaccinated – the circuits are too well integrated and the absorption of the evil is automatic.

In a sense the system wants absolutely to create its antithesis.

Yes, but there isn't one any more. We've devoured the antithesis. Even the antithesis has become a prosthesis.

And do you think such a phenomenon could occur in the USA?

There is an American fundamentalism. Analysing the Waco episode and the Oklahoma bombing, Gore Vidal shows that the fundamental antagonism, outside racial and economic conflicts, the real war of secession, is now between the individual – the typical product of American liberalism – and the federal state. This deep hostility to the state, which we have difficulty imagining here, has no doubt been there from the start. The state here is experienced as the emanation of a civil society, whereas over there it barely has any sovereignty, and the individual's always on the verge of feeling persecuted by it. This is the source of the fundamentalism of the whole American extreme Right, including that of the military circles. There's the potentiality in this for an internal terrorism, which has often been seen at work. Not an anti-American terrorism, but rather a hyper-American terrorism – a form of exacerbated isolationism. One imagines America as a kind of homogeneous superpower, but it isn't: as with everywhere else, there's this old visceral hostility to the universality of the state, that dominant abstraction of modern history. Is it a good, is it an evil? However this may be, the more the powers of the state are strengthened, the more this muted revolt grows, a revolt that isn't even exactly political, but calls into question the political structure. You might call it reactionary, from the standpoint of the dominant liberalism. Both in France and in the wider Europe, there is in this same way an anti-Europeanism that isn't met only among farmers or small traders – a rejection of this synthetic Europe and the abstract entity of Brussels.

A desire for singularity?

Yes, everything that resists global power today is part of that. It underlies all the forms of isolationism and ethnic, linguistic and religious particularism that resist this enforced promotion into the universal. Look what happened in the Dutch parliamentary elections of 2002. You have there a rich, enlightened, totally conformist country, a country so self-assured that it can afford itself the luxury of permissiveness (drugs, etc.). Well, suddenly, at the elections, deepest Holland went over to the extreme Right.

THE VACCINATED SYSTEM

Twin Holland?

Yes, the silent, perverse twin awakened. Suddenly, it was acting out, bursting out, like in *Alien*.

What you say about singularity is interesting, because in Argentina in recent years we've seen a kind of acting-out of singularity, but through failure – a pursuit of differentiation through failure. It may be thrilling, as you say, to feel privileged by bad luck, even by banal, rather than fateful, bad luck.

You can mark yourself out as singular by the best of things or the worst. Specificity can come through misfortune, provided it's out of the ordinary. But to go back to the Le Pen episode, there's an original twist here. It's no longer a protest from some part of the political chessboard, but a manifestation of an allergy to the political itself – and hence something almost transpolitical. The transversal emergence of something other, of an unidentified political object. In this sense, I'd like to rethink what happened in May '68 – to do so, that is, not in political, ideological terms or in terms of its consequences, but as an event, a ruptural event. And, paradoxically, May '68 arose out of a crisis of prosperity, and the moral poverty that ensued from economic prosperity. Prosperity faced people with a problem of changed values. The old prohibitions, the old miseries, were over and done with; the new challenge was how to come to terms with your needs, your desires, all your pleasures – and that's where things began to go wrong. An abreaction to what was called the consumer society, in fact to that sudden broadening of the horizon, to that form of de-territorialization, to the new lifestyle competition. That's what the universities reacted to first, in a kind of anticipated suicide of knowledge and culture. This all became diluted subsequently into economic demands, but that wasn't the real story. It was the mental fracture that was the key, and a defensive reaction to everything that was already looming as the future global order: a technical, free-market order. And there weren't any real political consequences to the event, nor any bright future to follow, but, at the time, there *was* an event, something mythic, which precisely flouted causes and consequences. All in all, we find ourselves facing a fracture of the same type today, that of a broadening to a global horizon, implicitly experienced as catastrophe . . .

But, since then, May '68 has been whitewashed . . .

Of course it has, just as the French Revolution was whitewashed by taking out the Terror. They found the 'correct' way of dealing with the Revolution. Where 1968 is concerned, since there was no means to find a 'correct' way of dealing with it, it's been consigned to the dustbins of history. This is quite simply revisionism, if not indeed historical denial. What hurts is the meaning *as event*, the implacable element that wells up in a society on the path to total reconciliation. So, the event has at all costs to be peacefully laid to rest, and its political exploitation primarily serves that end.

But the Le Pen episode didn't have the force of a pure event. It only went half way . . .

Yes, it was just a twist characteristic of a new type of event, of a new situation that has no parallel with political history or prehistory. In my opinion, the World Trade Center event's part of this too.

THE VACCINATED SYSTEM

It looks like an event destined never to take place. As in Waiting for Godot, *you're sure it won't happen, but everyone's waiting for it. And there's something in play in that waiting.*

Perhaps it's a form of silent plotting that corresponds in some way to the conspiracy between events (for events conspire together, we can be sure of that). It's perhaps a form of immunization too, of vaccination against catastrophe. At any rate, the relation between the 'real' or historical world and the world of events is very strange. They're two parallel universes that don't have the same co-ordinates. With historical violence, even revolutionary violence, even the Cold War, we were in a single dimension, whereas here, we're in an asymmetrical order that's no longer, strictly speaking, a history. In this sense, Fukuyama isn't entirely wrong: history as determination, history as such, is over. What's happening now no longer corresponds to a historical unity of space-time.

But surely you wouldn't agree with him . . . !

No, of course not. Not in his panegyric for the democratic, free-market system. But he does get some things right. For example, his judgement of French intellectuals. What is it with these intellectuals, he says, who swear by no one but Sade, Nietzsche and Artaud and sign democratic petitions for human rights or against war?

He finds this incoherent, that this metaphysical ferocity goes together with such political conformism . . .

And he's quite right. All these intellectually incorrect ideologues who have a politically correct unconscious (even if it expresses itself only in petitions or in a 'democratic' sensibility) – their references all subversive, their behaviour entirely compliant.

There seem to be two parallel universes: the universe of Good and Evil in capitals and that of good and evil lower-case. Nietzsche himself said that. You may feel beyond Good and Evil in capitals, but not at all beyond lower-case good and evil. In a word, you can transgress in upper case, while conforming in lower case.

I prefer Fukuyama, who, for his part, isn't concerned any longer with Good and Evil in capital letters and who advocates good without constantly eyeing evil. Take another example, that of Julia Kristeva! Talking of the Front National vote, she spoke of the French having an Unconscious that was complicit with Le Pen. Yet she must have some understanding of the Unconscious. She must know it's a total absurdity, from the pyschoanalytic standpoint, to make the Unconscious the obscure accomplice in a political act, for what would a political determination of the unconscious be? She knows all this, but when democratic morality demands it, she'll mobilize the Unconscious and prostitute it ideologically in the service of democracy. An easy solution, but a dangerous one, since then, at the same time as she's denouncing those who voted for Le Pen, she's also denouncing the Unconscious. Now, to denounce the Unconscious is ridiculous, as ridiculous as it would be to make the unconscious denounce something. A fine example of duplicity.

You've spoken of Latin America as an exciting phenomenon: it never seems able to find a political, economic or social reality principle, which represents an advantage today over the European confusion about these same principles. Might Latin America, paradoxically, have a more developed uncertainty principle than Europe?

The so-called underdeveloped countries are in the avant-garde in that sense: they've skipped the transition through all the phases of modernity in which we're currently bogged down. But my proposition mainly concerned Brazil. I find that in Brazil the categories of the economic or the political are hazier, more uncertain. Is it a question of societies that haven't yet incorporated the determining principles of the economic and the political, or societies that are already indeterministic, in which, with the rule today, as in the sciences, being uncertainty, social, economic and political categories are caught in this same uncertainty?

Could there be said to be a kind of de-stabilization of politics that hasn't first passed through stability?

Everyone's agreed on rescuing the imaginary of politics, but, in the end, the political has fallen into the sphere of the floating signifier, as Lévi-Strauss would say: a changeable, random space, as witness the fluctuations of Right and Left or the American elections, for example. This is all reinforced by opinion polls that claim to report on a hazy reality and are themselves even hazier than the reality.

Not so long ago, in Argentina, there was, concretely, a sort of sudden de-signification of signs – at the level of the institutions, but also of the economy. It's happened to us several times that money has lost its value – it had realized itself beyond the real in a sort of trance-like realization, in hyper-inflation. Furthermore, people lost their trust in the banks, everyone went to take out their money together. It's like a disappearance of the sign, a kind of advanced integral reality laboratory!

It's perhaps the highest stage of money. In Germany, I was given two 500-euro notes. I wasn't able to change them anywhere. Even the bank refused to exchange them for cash. I had to pay them into my account and transform them into virtual money before they'd give them back to me as real money. There's no faith in the money-sign any longer (though that itself is an abstraction); only the digital counts. At bottom, value, like signs, can now realize itself successfully only within a very narrow window. For things to circulate as quickly as possible, value must no longer have the time to realize itself, signs must no longer have the time to signify.

The Suffering of Stones

NOAILLES: *It's really the de-signification of the sign, of banking and money. And debt, too, which has lost the sign of obligation. We're getting rid of that completely.*

BAUDRILLARD: Ah, yes, since it reappears in the form of stocks and shares. There's no longer even any negative equivalence – what made a debt a debt.

Suffering falls into this same category: if we're becoming increasingly sensitive to it and if we're trying increasingly to eliminate it (and death too), that's because it has no equivalence any more and no value. You no longer suffer for a God, for your salvation, for another world – there, at least, there was a form of equivalence. Current suffering's unbearable because it no longer has an equivalent.

It seems every form of exchange with suffering has been forgotten except therapy. In fact, we could be said to have replaced all metaphysics by therapies capable of immediately expurgating the dissonances the universe might present. This is the new preventive metaphysics. Yet, what should be exchangeable for suffering seems also to be lacking!

Yes, and as a consequence, its exchange becomes doubly impossible. For that reason, too, I'm more sensitive to non-human suffering, to the suffering of animals or trees (not to mention the suffering of stones! Let's think of the specific, silent suffering of being a stone, or, in other words, in Heidegger's terms, of not even being-in-the-world!). I feel this not out of ecological sensibility, but because human suffering, for its part at least, has its equivalence in a consciousness – that's why it was once the only suffering that moved us, because it was the only form that could speak and represent itself. But today, the suffering of inanimate entities has become more moving, because they don't even have a destiny; they don't even have the right of moral retribution for their suffering. So, it's even more unjust – if that term can indeed have a sense elsewhere than in human consciousness. What's changing, too, is that we're falling into the same inhuman condition, that of beings without consciousness that suffer for nothing. With no possible equivalence. We are, then, becoming more sensitive to what is happening on the other side, the inhuman side. Where misfortune is concerned, we're seeing a whole system of equivalence and compensation being created: the whole victim syndrome that's thriving everywhere. To have yourself recognized as a victim is one of your human rights today. There's a whole political economy of misfortune. There is a possible exchange of misfortune, whereas there's no possible exchange of evil.

There's a vertiginous – and almost inhuman – beauty in what you've just said. This might be seen as a turn on the part of the universe towards absolute gratuitousness, a kind of moral unemployment in which we've lost the right to a minimum social income. A voluntary unemployment, as it were, and you prefer the universe of all that we've always considered as slavish, the inhuman universe, to these new unemployed, who want, moreover, to liberate it. (All that's missing is the liberation of stones indeed.) As for exchange, this is the distinction we were talking about before between evil and misfortune . . .

Evil is this extreme situation of impossible exchange. The world is unexchangeable because there's no criterion of equivalence external to the world. This radical situation is unbearable, and hence a convertible situation has to be substituted for it: that of misfortune. Misfortune is exchangeable, and hence bearable, the ideal being that everything should be soluble in exchange. This puts me in mind of a film, Charles Najman's *Can Memory Dissolve in Évian Water?*, in which you see Auschwitz survivors taking the waters at a spa every year in the lap of luxury, all paid for by the Germans. They are, at bottom, going back to the primal scene of the camp: what they went through then, they are reliving in the mode of reconciliation. Most of them are very pleased with this. In reality, they've found the solution to the impossible exchange of death.

It's rather like the idea that suffering in this life will be compensated else-where. But, in fact, it's like a doubling of the suffering. It's a strange make-over – underscoring the past like this with its sign reversed.

Yes, evil is made over into misfortune. Evil is soluble in misfortune. That's what 'victimhood' is.

Could you range this idea of evil and misfortune under that of tragedy? For example, when Clément Rosset says that misfortune begins only when you no longer accept the real? Misfortune might be said to begin when you think things could have been different.

Yes, *ressentiment* is the product of an – inevitably – disappointed idealization. Cioran says, for example, that it's the desire to give a meaning to life that makes us failures. But where Rosset's concerned, there's an ambiguity over the meaning of the term 'real'. He employs it in a radical sense, that of an absolute 'idiocy' [*idiotie*], which for me would be the equivalent of singularity. But I agree with him on the aura of the real 'in itself', stripped of any interpretation, whether it be that of music or Camembert: every-thing's idiomatic. What remains strange is that we strive remorselessly to disenchant this singular object, to pervert the real, precisely by giving it meaning.

So, any inclination to change the world is necessarily inspired by unhappiness or misfortune?

It's both the engine and the ineluctable consequence of changing the world. From the standpoint of evil, there's no sense wanting to change the world.

Perhaps this standpoint of evil has been obscurely understood, that it's senseless to want to change the world. This would solve the mystery of Marx's thesis on Feuerbach ('Hitherto existing philosophers have merely interpreted the world, the point, however, is to change it'). And that would absolve us philosophers at a stroke! (But who will absolve us of interpretation?)

To change the world is to finalize it: we're still in the phantasm of surpassing and perfection here – a phantasm that automatically fuels unhappiness. How do things work? Do they work according to the law, according to reason? There would, in that case, be some chance of reducing evil, and we wouldn't need misfortune. But, in fact, everyone uses this latter immorally, and societies themselves, according to Mandeville, function by illegality and corruption. It seems that's where the vital energy lies – or at least the rules of the social game. Do we have to call this corruption? That's about as justified as calling everything in our psychical lives that contravenes the moral law 'perversion'. It's law and order that can be termed perverse. The symbolic form, for its part, the rules of the game, are never perverse.

This is evil showing through in an order that sees itself as the order of good. And here we get to a supra-sensible, supra-moral position which reveals that no one ultimately has ever regarded the moral law as something written in the hearts of men. The moral law is a bit like the social order; it's an epiphenomenon, a fragile, exceptional structure under constant challenge. In fact, evil is always there, like the void beyond space.

And everyone has a grasp of evil, without necessarily being aware of it. With misfortune, on the other hand, everyone's aware of it; it's an object of exchange, understanding, solidarity and conviviality. It circulates like an official commodity (whereas evil tends, rather, to circulate on the black market); but behind this banal exchange, this statistical equivalence of misfortune, there's doubtless the insight into another order, an order without possible equivalence, that of evil. Other societies made the distinction clearly, recognizing duality, which, for us, has become the absolute heresy, whereas in those societies, there was no heresy, but a ritual, sacrificial putting-in-play of that duality.

Of irreconcilement?

Yes. But we're no longer in a dual order; we're in a dialectical order and under the principle of reconciliation. On the question of the irreconcilable, they've just discovered Neanderthal man to be an 'other' human species. Other in the sense that it couldn't reproduce with our own, *Homo sapiens*. This duality is interesting. It's even a fantastic scenario, the idea that there were *two* human species, one of which, the Neanderthal, disappeared after 15,000 years of cohabitation in the same European space. This means that since the other was eliminated, we've retained a monopoly on the human, and on a unidirectional anthropology. That should cast some ambiguity on the concepts of the human and humanism.

Neanderthal Man

NOAILLES: *But the monopoly is itself growing tired. With cloning, we're rediscovering the lost duplicity.*

BAUDRILLARD: Perhaps that's the unhappy destiny of all that manages to establish itself as sole possessor of a power, whatever it may be. Monopoly is unstable. It's doomed to split or fracture. We saw this with the Cold War, where things operated around two poles under the sign of the balance of terror. Once the monopoly of global power was achieved, after communism had fallen, that global power fractured and was confronted with its monstrous double: terrorism in all its forms. *Our* double – you're right – is the clone. Oneness, giving birth on its own, produces a simulacrum of itself or a double. Cloning might thus be said to be a kind of miscarriage. Yet, we're moving towards this oneness, this totality, by the elimination of all singularities, such as that of this twin, different human race.

This is very interesting because, with clones, we're recreating this twinness melancholically.

A system that's exterminated the other can only be exterminated in return. It ends up producing this rebound of the selfsame destroying itself – a kind of esoteric disaster.

We're perhaps in a world that knows it seems to have lost its own shadow, that knows it's lost the light source that gave rise to that shadow, and that's desperately seeking to regenerate it by way of duplication. Might this head-long flight forward be the product of fear of the revenge of this exterminated shadow; the product of the presentiment of an inevitable duel, like that of William Watson in Poe's tale? In that case, as at Samarkand once again, a fateful destiny awaits us. Out of fear of the vengeance of the proscribed shadow, we're producing a world whose hidden function will be precisely to avenge that shadow. Could the clone be said, then, to be a kind of suicide of the species? And what would the obsessive fear be that leads us to cloning?

A complex, derivative form of mortality, whereas cloning was intended to ensure automatic immortality for us. What are we seeking? Precisely this perpetual identity, this definitive form. But splitting oneself indefinitely is a way of going over to the other side, beyond one's own end.

But we might also suspect that when the infinite of a situation is eliminated absolutely, when only the finite remains, that tends to vanish into the infinite.

Yes, it's the splitting of the finite into another infinite. But this self-multiplication is interpreted as a progress towards the universal, which is entirely wrong. We're sacrificing the prey for its shadow, the universal for the global. Which is, perhaps, a remote consequence of the fact that, to safeguard that universal, we've sacrificed others: the Neanderthal, for example. If there are two different human species, there's no universality. When one of the two is eliminated, the remaining one becomes universal. That was how we became the sole and unique universal human being! – at the risk of becoming Neanderthals again, or seeing them re-emerge. For we still are secretly a little Neanderthal. The spectre of the Neanderthal is always there!

All that's been repressed, all that's been eradicated, carries on obscurely along its parallel path. We carry it within ourselves like the dead twins in mythologies. Of the two twins, there's always one who has to die. But he's still there, inside, and life is an immense labour of de-twinning. I have my own little theory, on the fringes of psychoanalysis, about the fundamental separation. It isn't the separation from parents, but the break with one's original twin. In the beginning, we're always two, and we have to get rid of our twin. And we only really exist from the moment we get rid of him. It's very difficult. Some never manage it. There's always this buried otherness or, rather, buried 'sameness', and all problems of identity, of neurosis, come much more profoundly from this breaking of twinness or the failure of that break, than from the parental drama.

I like this 'theory': perhaps the labour of a life consists in washing away the bloodstains of this sacrifice. It's the term of the duality that was eliminated that becomes your destiny.

It resurfaces involuntarily, one way or another. If you eliminate it, you find yourself with countless twins (clones are an illustration of this) – a teeming twinness which is simply the endless metastasis of the being that was eliminated at the beginning. So, all the virtual egos eliminated at birth by the constitution of a single ego – all these other egos – make up our profound otherness.

Either you respect duality, so to speak, even lost duality, or you create a unity that metastasizes.

Unless you manage to bring twinness back into play. But almost all the stories of mythological twins have a tragic ending. It's a destiny that leads, one way or another, to death. We choose to eliminate one of them from the outset, which brings us back to Neanderthal man, who seems like the monstrous twin we really had to get rid of. Today, when we can no longer pride ourselves so assuredly on the universality acquired at his expense, we're turning back to him with some nostalgia, as we are to all the cultures or species that have been sacrificed. Retrospectively, we're no longer very sure of the universality of the human race, but it's no use mourning, since we are, in any case, going to offload it on to an artificial species that won't even remember it.

Why do we experience duality as a threat, but not the oneness that splits or metastasizes?

All the ethical problems around cloning show that it's felt to be a threatening prospect and, at the same time, exerts a fascination more powerful than any morality. We have to come back here to the distinction between seduction and fascination. Fascination is linked to vertigo. And the technical transformation of the world, of which the reduplication of the species is part, is a vertiginous undertaking. Chain reactions and the exponential are fascinating. Seduction is, by contrast, a dual game, a finite game, with rules. It has its measure; it has its limits; it stands opposed to the modern universe of deregulation. Fascination is linked to the desire for immortality which the whole development of technology implies, whereas seduction implies death. Now that we're set on this vertiginous course today, I can't see what could be ranged against it.

I don't see anything emerging from elsewhere to get the better of this irreversible process. Out of what's currently becoming the 'all', I can't see where the 'nothing' might re-emerge. But, in fact, the more we press forward with the duplication of human beings, the more we notice they're incredibly ambivalent, and we can't reproduce that ambivalence. The more we press on with the transformation of the world, the more we notice it's the world itself that resists globalization. Oneness and duality: it's an endless pursuit race around the Moebius strip.

So humanity seems to have invented the real only so as to have illusion always before it, as destiny? It seems to have eliminated its twin in order to ensure a destiny – even a fatal destiny - for itself? Might it have eliminated its twin only to ensure that, if ever it had nothing to pursue, it would at least be secretly pursued by someone? At any rate, this pursuit race around the Moebius strip is precisely what makes it difficult to imagine illusion being eliminated.

The more we hunt it down, the more it infiltrates, like a virus, into the very interior of the process. And this is reassuring, since it signifies the *a priori* failure of any systematic attempt at disillusionment.

And how does this self-splitting of the global monopoly play itself out at the political level? What's the equivalent of cloning at the political level?

It's the establishment of a political and cultural order generative of millions of clones – not necessarily genetically, but mentally cloned, and programmatically differentiated. We've already reached this point. And this fractalization of the same model also applies in politics, which also reproduces itself clonally by way of opinion polls, statistics, stifling consensual thinking and political double-speak. In the end, this will become an immense theme park in which democratic individualization will generate a Brownian motion of elementary particles and free radicals, each becoming the clone of the other and, most importantly, of itself. What we may hope is that all of this will unleash some new passions, a whole mimetic violence, a virulence of mimetic desire, once there comes to be rivalry between each individual and his double. *The Student of Prague* can serve as a reference here, that film in which the student's double, put into circulation by the devil, precedes the student everywhere he goes, anticipating his acts and his least desires.

In another age, the psychoanalyst Otto Rank saw doubling as an ancestral fear of death, with the double representing what protects us from our own death. Fears have transmuted into fascination, and the double now has the function of hastening death. So is it like a sort of secret urge? Does a universe expurgated of its shadow (and its death) exert an absolute fascination? As Heraclitus said: 'How will one hide from that which never sets?'[21]

Let's take matter: when you begin to analyse it, you move towards simpler and simpler elements, invisible, elusive particles, towards that which no longer has any reference to matter as substance. It's the same with the

---

[21] This is Diels–Kranz fragment number 16, cited here after Charles H. Kahn, *The Art and Thought of Heraclitus*, (Cambridge: Cambridge University Press, 1987), p. 271. Kahn's full translation reads: 'How will one hide from (*lathoi*: 'escape the notice of') that which never sets?'

human: we've begun to split it, break it up, reduce it to simple elements, to the point of genetic exploration, the mapping of the genome – a point where there's no longer any human referent. There's no more of a human referent in current genetics than there's a material referent in subatomic physics.

Perhaps this process is, secretly, of the order of the instinct of repetition . . .

Yes, of machinic accounting. Let's take the example of *The Sexual Life of Catherine M.* It's the story of a machinic sexual investigation, of a mechanics of sex and copulation, free of any seduction and desire. Does this still have anything to do with sex? No, it has to do precisely with repetition, with functional repetition identically and to infinity. This is why I posed the question whether Catherine M. was really a sexed being.

It might be said, rather, to be the cloning of sex. But there are other machinic behaviours than the sexual.

Yes, and I very well understand the desire to be a machine, to go to the limits of machinality. And, ultimately, cloning is just the human version of seriality,[22] the modern dimension of the industrial world, and, subsequently, of the artistic world. Warhol illustrated this brilliantly with his 'machinic snobbery'. Machinality is an original event, but immediately afterwards it becomes just that – a machinic event, a purely repetitive mechanics, expressing that

---

[22] 'la version humaine de la sérialité'. There are overtones here of 'mass production', which, in French, is 'la production en série'.

yearning for repetition which Freud saw as the death drive. And we find ourselves up against the same question: Is seriality a way of putting an end to the image? Is repetitive sex a way of putting an end to sex (and seduction)? Is cloning a way of putting an end to the original (the human being)? We can see Catherine M. only as a sexually indifferent being, indefinitely miming sexuality, giving all the conventional signs of sexual activity. There's an unexpected destiny of 'liberated' sexuality here. And it is, in fact, a question of liberation. The liberation of sex sets it free to repeat itself indefinitely, just as the liberation of work sets human beings free to work indefinitely. Just as, for its part, reproduction, liberated from sexuality by cloning, also assumes limitless dimensions.

Perhaps it's the horror at having lost sex that leads to its being continually verified . . .

Yes, it's by dint of sex that Catherine M. establishes the indifference of the sexual act, while at the same time according it an exclusive value. It's almost as though she were cheating on herself sexually. This view of sex as ultimate illumination, that is to say, as an illumination that puts an end to sex itself, is really an eschatological belief [*une croyance des derniers jours*] – a kind of libidinal *parousia*, contemporaneous with the subsumption of all forms of action into machinality.

It's the Inhuman that Thinks Us

NOAILLES: *Some points in* Simulacra and Simulation *have never reappeared subsequently, or have perhaps reappeared in another form. I'm thinking of the problem of the 'remainder'. You listed the dialectical oppositions: only with the remainder was there nothing on the other side of the bar. Nothing stands opposed to the remainder. You wrote: 'When a system has absorbed everything, when one has added everything up, when nothing remains, the entire total changes into the remainder, becomes remainder'.[23] The idea is perhaps an anticipation of impossible exchange, as it's a kind of unexchangeable principle that cannot accede to value.*

BAUDRILLARD: It's like the nothing. The nothing's perfect because it's opposed to nothing (it isn't opposed to the 'all', the 'everything'; it's something else). The remainder isn't opposed to anything; it has no contrary (except perhaps the surplus, the opposite of the residue?). But the problem of what has no opposite is much wider than this: it's the general problem of singularity. The apple has no opposite, this table has no opposite, this poem has no opposite. This apple, then, is perfect, this table is perfect, since they are opposed to nothing.

Yes, the singularity is opposed to nothing so long as it isn't dragged towards a dialectical form, so long as it doesn't move away from a form of dual exchange. The world is a singularity that couldn't be said to be opposed to thought, but rather poses a challenge to it. This is what makes it possible to say that it's the world that thinks us, like the mirror in The Seducer's Diary:[24]

---

[23] Jean Baudrillard, *Simulacra and Simulation*, trans. Sheila Faria Glaser (Ann Arbor: University of Michigan Press, 1994), p. 144; trans. modified.

[24] Søren Kierkegaard, 'The Seducer's Diary', in *Either/Or*, Part I, ed. and translated by Howard V. Hong and Edna H. Hong (Princeton: Princeton University Press, 1987), pp. 301–445.

IT'S THE INHUMAN THAT THINKS US

Cordelia doesn't think of the mirror, but the mirror thinks of her. That thought is akin also to the idea that it's language that thinks us, that it's language that speaks through us.

Yes, and also it's television that watches us, and so on. A paradoxical game of subject–object inversion that means just one simple thing: we believe we think the world, but the belief is mutual. It's a dual relation, and we can think it only because it thinks us in return. And this isn't in any way a question of interactivity; it isn't a question-and-answer or communication game.

It's a challenge, without either sender or receiver . . .

Yes, each one sizes the other up. Each has an understanding with the other. It's a rivalrous complicity. We aren't talking, then, of objective knowledge, nor of thought as logical organization. I don't know how to define what thinking means in this sense. The closest illustration for me is photography. There I have the distinct impression, more than in the field of writing, that it's the world that sees me and makes itself seen. The shot's a two-way process. But that's the very essence of the gaze: either it's a two-way thing or it's nothing.

It's a kind of intersection between two agencies in flight: neither the subject nor the world is what it was any more. It isn't an inversion either.

No, it isn't a pure and simple inversion of the privilege of the object. It's more of the order of what Plato says about the image: the image is at the intersection of the light coming from the object and that coming from the gaze.

That's amazing! Is that in Plato?

I hope so. Otherwise, it'll join the fake quotations!

Like Ecclesiastes?

Yes, like the quotation from *Ecclesiastes* (the epigraph to *Simulacra and Simulation*: 'The simulacrum is never what hides the truth – it is truth that hides the fact that there is none. The simulacrum is true.'[25] There is, of course, no such verse in *Ecclesiastes*). This phrase – 'it's the world that thinks us' – is a bit like those poetic phrases we were talking about. It isn't really susceptible of commentary. But it isn't mystical, it's simply enigmatic.

You see it even better perhaps with language. Ultimately, we can understand the world as language, and when we say, 'the world that thinks us', we would in fact be saying, 'language that traverses us'.

[25] Baudrillard, *Simulacra and Simulation*, p. 1.

Do you mean by that what Nietzsche says: that it's language – grammar, syntax, the subject, the complement, plural, singular, etc. – that shapes our value system and governs our morality?

The idea of the world as language goes even further: it's a kind of unsaid verbality; it's the blossoming of appearances. I can clearly see how language is extra-human, even if, at some particular time, it takes a human form. The human being might thus be said to be a hollow form through which language itself blows, and the whole task would consist, then, in modulating that void to give form to this sound. So, when Heraclitus says in the famous fragment 50, 'It is wise, listening not to me but to the report [τού λόγου], to agree that all things are one,' he's saying there's something elsewhere one hears, there's something elsewhere that speaks – and that is language. It's the unsaid that speaks, and we reply. Yet, in order to reply and in order for the duel to exist, we should speak, while at the same time retaining a kind of non-saying. But it's difficult (and, at the same time, beautiful) to transpose this same inversion on to thought itself.

What's difficult to conceive is a subjectless thought, a non-reflecting thought. Thought is conventionally of the order of reflection. So when we say, 'it's the world that thinks us', this is precisely to get around the trap of the subject thinking the world when he reflects, in a position of mastery, as the subject of knowledge. Now, thought is something different from – human, all too human – reflection; it is, rather, the refraction of what there is that's inhuman in the world. We might equally well say: it's the inhuman that thinks us. At any rate, it is in fact a duel, and in this dual circuit of thought there's no privileged position – and doubtless not even any determinate position at all. And the language that circulates from the one to the other is, to go back to Plato's formula, at the meeting-point of the human and the inhuman.

If it isn't overturning privileges, it is, at any rate, abolishing our *privilege.*

Certainly. Other systems of thought, other cultures don't have any philosophy in the reflective sense of the term. They're content simply to name things, to describe a kind of mental space in which forms circulate: you are not truly anywhere, but you are in the succession of that which is said. Thought in this sense is akin to poetry.

If thought is the refraction of what's inhuman in the world, we might be said to be back perhaps to the idea of prism. Thought would be the surface of incidence and of deviation of the light of the world, of its conversion and decomposition. Yet, as you say, language (light) circulates from the one to the other, and the world might be said to act in the same way, deviating and decomposing any interpretation, without for all that abandoning the challenge of thought. It would be a kind of encounter, without any form of adaequatio. *This raises a question: how would concepts be born? Foucault says man was invented 200 years ago. In other words, there wasn't any 'man' before; it's an invention of language. Even better, as Heidegger said, in Greek there are no objects; the Greeks don't have 'culture', 'religion' or 'social relations'. And of course, one might add, Oedipus didn't have an Oedipus complex at all!*

To conceive this form, we'd have to abandon the transcendent logic that dreams of decoding the world, of discovering the secret key to it held somewhere. Immanent logic intensifies the enigma and is opposed, in fact, to the diminishing of the world's secrets and the idea that things are waiting to be discovered. But the world isn't enciphered: it is said in the only way possible, without translation, explanation or development. (This reminds me of Pessoa's phrase: 'Things are the only hidden meaning of things.') Or, to paraphrase T. S. Eliot, if things had had another way of expressing themselves, they'd have expressed themselves differently. Ultimately, the fact of perceiving the world as a woman slipping what is hidden beneath her skirts is what has always justified the ravishing of the world. You can always argue that 'the world led me on'. Concepts aren't fixed, waiting to be discovered by an expanding wisdom; they emerge from a sort of intersection between language and the world. We can't be said to be faced with a world of latencies which yield themselves to knowledge by a slow strip-tease, but a world in which the irruption of language has a power of instantiation.

We've naively forced language to bite the dust of linearity; we've forced things to bite the dust of finality. But the linear transforms itself, like any supporting material; it's too fine a silk, it's a material that collapses when you apply an excessive load of meaning to it. Like language, which isn't that homogeneous surface we'd like it to be, the world, which isn't such a surface either, yields with a sudden intensity, paralysed by the obligation to stay still. The real, subject to this kind of sexual harassment, feigns a climax, thus allowing the univocal interpretative discourses to feel like good lovers. But this demand for increasing, simulated jouissance *exhausts all interpretation and renders it impotent . . .*

We may ask ourselves what manipulation causes a man-effect, a subject-effect, a reality-effect, a history-effect, to emerge from language? Even in the case of the Unconscious, when Freud coins that term, something begins truly to exist. Far from being a timeless psychical structure, the Unconscious begins at that point. And this moment of conceptual invention is a critical threshold where things, reflected by the word that names them, both assume force of reality and begin to fade.

This happens perhaps when language is operating with a will to reflection, which would, in reality, render it refractory. Although language could also have the power to name as well as to denominate . . .

The Genealogy of Disappearance

BAUDRILLARD: It's the beginning of the end, if I may put it like that. Things are realized by language and, at the same time, short-circuited by it. The class struggle, for example: when Marx enunciates the concept, when that concept surfaces in historical consciousness, the unbridled phase of the class struggle is already at an end. 'When I speak of time, it already is no more,' said Apollinaire.[26] This is difficult to grasp, because the common conception has it that it's at this point, in fact, that the story begins. But the genesis and destiny of ideas are more complex. Reality exists through language; then, within the shadow of language, it quietly ceases to exist. Doubtless it's the same with the very recent concept of globalization, which has itself suddenly gone global. Mightn't this sudden spread of the concept mean that globalization is, to all intents and purposes, over and that we're moving on to something else now?

NOAILLES: *I like this idea: things materialize and come to their end, as it were. Hegel suspected this too: philosophy appears only when reality has accomplished and terminated its process of formation. It's only as twilight descends that the owl of Minerva flies out.*

---

[26] I have not been able to locate this line in Apollinaire, though it does occur in Raymond Queneau's poem 'Les Ziaux'.

THE GENEALOGY OF DISAPPEARANCE

Globalization's been around for a long time – in business, finance, culture, drugs, mores, music and pornography (doubtless the first case of 'global' expansion). What's new is that the concept has been invented (and, in the process, that of anti-globalization). The invention of the concept is a decisive moment – that of the Unconscious in Freud's work, for example, or of the class struggle in Marx. But this moment of emergence is also the moment it begins to disappear, the beginning of the end of what it denotes. It's like philosophy for Hegel, which appears at twilight. Are we already at the twilight of globalization? The seal would be set on the apogee of globalization, then, by the event marking its end – namely, the destruction of the Twin Towers, which were its emblem. An event that occurred not long after the advent of the concept. Just as the fall of the Berlin Wall ushered in the end of a certain history – precisely that history that preceded the 'global' era. But what new situation does the event of 11 September usher in? It's a paradoxical fact: as soon as they're hallowed by the concept – in other words, as nominal values – all these things vanish as realities. At the point where they become the leitmotif or obligatory reference of a culture, they're already disappearing. Values shine out only as they are waning, and sometimes even, like dead stars, their light reaches us only when they no longer exist. Thought too, like Kafka's Messiah, always arrives late. This is the destiny of value (economic, moral or political). After the moment of their general acceptance, which was the moment of the universal, in which they were underwritten by a kind of gold reserve and transcendent equivalence, they fall into the ecstasy of value, where they're no longer exchangeable for anything, but circulate increasingly rapidly and revolve faster and faster on their orbit: this is the paroxystic stage in which all values become indistinguishable. We could subject sexuality to the same analysis. Once it's being named and identified everywhere, it's in its terminal phase.

It may be that the fact of naming is the most secret form of the rear-view mirror (McLuhan said that an era thought only through its rear-view mirror). Might language be a form of despair about what is disappearing, while at the same time being an agent of that disappearance? Does language, like the world, hover between the retrieval of what is disappearing and the annihilation of what sees itself as unilaterally real?

In that sense, history too is something we project retrospectively. All these founding concepts are founded only on the names that articulate them. It's a kind of genealogy of disappearance. This connects also with what Lacan said about language: that it isn't what conveys meaning, but what's there in place of meaning. We think, naively, that where there's language there's meaning, whereas, when language comes into being, meaning is no longer really there. (And the converse is true: when meaning wins out, language is no longer there.)

Perhaps it's the emptiness of something that calls on language to name it; when it nears its end, it's the emptiness that proposes . . .

. . . and language that disposes. In other words, it's when things disappear that you seek to verify them, that the whole machinery of verification through language gets going. And the more you verify, the more reality fades. It's a paradoxical, perverse effect of which reason knows nothing. It knows only how to prove and provide evidence. But that within truth which is only truth is of the order of illusion. Things present their credentials through language. But that merely holds up a mirror to their disappearance.

There are two wagers. The first, as we were saying before, is that all the big concepts – the unconscious, history, etc. – are invented; they aren't discovered. But your argument goes even further: by the time language arrives, what it names has already disappeared.

When something is reflected and from the moment it's reflected, the fact is that it's no longer being thought. Where thought ends, reflection begins. This connects with Borges's fable, 'Fauna of Mirrors'.[27] A fantastic fable: the defeated peoples are condemned by the Empire to be imprisoned behind mirrors, where they merely reflect the image of their conquerors. But one day they begin to resemble them less and less, and in the end, they pass through to the other side of the mirror and invade the Empire . . .

It's a story of silent revolt.

It's the whole story of representation. Those who are condemned to resemblance and representation are the defeated. Representation is a slave condition. To free yourself, you must smash the mirror of representation. Behind every image, behind every representation, behind every concept perhaps, there's a defeated person, someone who's disappeared – but who isn't dead and who's waiting for the point where they'll no longer be a likeness, no longer a mere reflection, and will re-emerge victorious.

[27] Jorge Luis Borges, 'Fauna of Mirrors', in *The Book of Imaginary Beings* (Harmondsworth: Penguin, 1974), pp. 67–8.

But it's the politicians themselves who long ago merrily kissed representation goodbye!

That's true. The Empire itself, the system, no longer functions by representation. But this duel between representation or reflection and thought – this last being beyond any reflecting – still exists.

So, apart from being one of the world's primordial forms, language might itself merely be the mirror of what has disappeared. Or perhaps a retarding mirror . . .

Yes, a consigning of things to house arrest in their very concepts, in the language that names them. And the Emperor would be something like the Master of language. Yet, language itself may disappear, with the appearance of digital languages – and the mirror itself disappear, with the appearance of the screen.

If the reflected form disappeared, it would no longer be possible even to smash the mirror. Are we talking about a disappearance of another order here, an extermination?

Yes, it's the end of the interplay between the world and thought, the interplay between the world and language. With the virtual stage of the screen, which eliminates the mirror stage, the world and language disappear simultaneously. What's in danger is this distancing function that belongs to language, this function of distinguishing itself from materiality by way of the concept and yet still being a fragment of the world, of the material world, this extraordinary paradoxical conjunction (there being no ascendancy of the one over the other, but a reciprocity between them). With digital and systemic organization, we're in a *dispositif* that's no longer even representational, but purely operational.

But which is, in a sense, another materialization of language.

Yes, admittedly, but in extremely simple elements, which are no longer signs, but ciphers. An inert world that responds to you now only with sterilized information, that is to say, information expurgated of any connotation of affect or meaning. From this point on, exchange is really impossible, but this world, the virtual world, no longer asks itself the question of impossible exchange: it has swallowed its own mirror; it has swallowed its own reference; it is its own truth. No transcendence any more, and hence no questioning. We're really up against what Hegel called 'a life of death, moving within itself'.[28] And which, of course, may continue indefinitely, since it is beyond distances, beyond contradictions. Now, language is what maintains distance. Language is so designed that you can't say everything at the same time. With the computer, the total logic tool,[29] by contrast, we have the possibility of saying everything at the same time, of simultaneously carrying out all operations. Hence, it's the absolute opposite of language. There's no longer any

[28] I have followed the translation here by the eminent Hegel scholar Shlomo Avineri in *Hegel's Theory of the Modern State* (London: Cambridge University Press, 1972), p. 95.
[29] The French is *logiciel*, a term which can normally be translated as 'software package', but which has broader connotations here.

negative, any distance. Everything can follow on by mere contiguity . . . But I'm a little distrustful of my own personal, subjective judgement in this matter, since that's a world that's alien to me . . .

I use it a lot. It's like a parallel universe that doesn't nullify thought, but I understand what you say. As in the case of clones, it is perhaps the dream of creating a language that obeys us completely . . .

What strikes me in all this is that you're there in front of your screen and you make everything appear on that screen. You call things up, and they come. All information's there, stored up; it's just waiting to be made available to you. It's exactly the opposite of the conception I might have of frequenting the world, of the emergence of the world, of the possibility of things happening or not happening, the kinds of surprises and events you've no control over. The idea that freedom means having everything available to you is a total misconception. Paradoxically, when everything's possible, and because everything's possible, I see this as the end of all sovereignty, both the world's and my own. Moreover, this incessant circulation, which corresponds to a mental immobilism, also has a counterpart at the physical level in a devastating immobilization of the body. The spectral body of the virtual is itself virtual; it no longer is a body. At the screen, the body's useless. The only beings adequate to this system of functioning are clones, automata or robots, since there's no need to be a human being to do this, and you no longer even should be.

Might we speak here of another 'mirror people'?

Absolutely. With this perfect obedience to the cybernetic command, we're back precisely at Borges's fable, but transposed now from mirror to screen. It's no longer the forced resemblance of the mirror, it's the total obedience and total virtual jurisdiction of the screen. And, to stay with the fable, we might ask what disappears, defeated, behind the screen, like the 'mirror people'? What, in virtual reality, has succumbed and been condemned to exile (having perhaps, unlike in the fable, no chance of re-emerging)? What is assigned, not in this case to resemblance and representation, but to virtuality and spectrality, to immediate presence in real time (on the screens) and unlimited duplication (cloning, which is the limitless form of resemblance and of the human in the age of its technical reproducibility, to parody Benjamin!)? There's an illustration of this in a recent news story. Someone put a small ad. on the Net. He was looking for a man of a particular height, particular appearance, particular eye and hair colour – precisely his own personal characteristics. He was looking for his twin, his double, his clone. Through the network, he found him – and killed him. He thus afforded himself the luxury of disappearing with impunity (he wanted to disappear, and he had to be believed to be dead). Cloning thus enables you to commit 'virtual' suicide; it enables you to survive while fleeing from yourself. Where this absorption of the human into the virtual screen is concerned, you've only to look at the postmistresses, the post office clerks behind their computers. They used to carry out manual, even mental, operations. Now, they each have their screen. The discrepancy between the two – the computers and these human beings – is incredible, for they're still human beings, but they're consigned to virtuality, in the same way as Borges's peoples are made to resemble their masters. So, to escape becoming mere extensions of the machines and to stay alive, they think up all kinds of things. They put flowers on their terminals. But it's like weeping over their own graves.

Polychrony

NOAILLES: *Just as language lies between two forms of non-existence ('Reality exists through language; then, within the shadow of language, it quietly ceases to exist'), might it be that thought lies between the non-existence of precession and that of realization? In any event, this time gap between thought and event could be related to the relative velocities of the world or, in other words, of time. 'True' time, which isn't the same for everything, which, unlike 'real time', isn't the time of absolute simultaneity, but the time that delays things and causes them not to coincide.*

BAUDRILLARD: Here again, time is what makes everything not happen at the same time, and it can even become a reversible dimension . . . Beyond chronological time and real time, one might envisage a singular time, the time of singularity. Physics already teaches us that every object has its own specific time and space. So, each singularity has its own time within which everything is synchronous and reversible, and the thought included in this event time may very well echo the event before its occurrence. Being in a time bubble is like being in a poem – another singularity where everything corresponds in all directions. A form of polychrony, if you like, which makes possible this reversion of thought to the event, and of the event to thought.

Yes, this can be seen clearly with poems, because the lines correspond and cast light on each other reciprocally, whether they're at the beginning or the end. There's a simultaneous light cast in all directions and you might say that

116

the notions of beginning and end lose their meaning, even though the organization of the poem is entirely rigorous. It's more or less the same with thought and the event you were speaking of. Perhaps everything's there from the outset, in the initiatory state, and this enables all directions to be kept open.

In language, too, all the possibilities are there, but it takes a form of accident for them to be brought into existence. The origin and the end are there simultaneously. Everything's there simultaneously in terms of vision (not of representation). It's more or less what Lévi-Strauss said about language. He advanced the very metaphysical hypothesis that, as signifying form, language appears in its entirety at a stroke. There's no primitive accumulation of language. It's a pure event. It's like thought. There's no primitive accumulation of thought. It doesn't appear over a process of evolution. Or even life, living matter: its appearance isn't the fruit of a long process of selection and adaptation. You can of course, trace the history and genealogy of life, but as a form it's there from the outset in its entirety, like the articulation of language. After that, you can produce meaning in ever greater quantities; you can follow all the twists and turns of signification; but, as event, meaning is there – virtually *ex nihilo*. And it's in this way, as form, that it's in danger of abruptly disappearing, as suddenly as it appeared. Once again, none of this has anything to do with the accumulation of knowledge; it's a question of how you see thought. In this view, it wouldn't be a reflective articulation but a kind of predestination that linked thought to the event, and the world to thought.

The drastic possibility you speak of here, of a sudden disappearance of language, is very interesting. Might language be battling against its own

disappearance by accomplishing the uninterrupted task of consigning every-
thing, in turn, to disappearance? Now, the relative velocities of things mean
they do not meet – which would be paradoxical if everything were there from
the outset.

Yes, there would be a risk of total confusion, of crowding and madness.

Perhaps this is another feature of illusion we can't bear: this total presence
of appearances, this absolute simultaneity . . . We have, then, to digest it, and
defer it.

Illusion has to be, or has to become, a game. And for it to be a 'putting in
play', a kind of dispersal's needed, a diffraction of appearances, as with white
light . . . The 'prismatics' you spoke of at the beginning.

Yes, the dispersive role of the prism being to separate the diversity of lights
that make up white light. To come back to the problem of time, you've
propounded the notion of real time as a kind of fourth dimension of time in
which the others are abolished. It's the dimension of the virtual that precedes
and substitutes for the real. What are the consequences of living in real time?

I don't know, I don't live in real time yet. Nor do I live exactly in the 'real
world' – and I certainly don't live in the instantaneous time of communica-
tions. I have a spontaneous form of resistance, or rather of allergy and indifference, that comes from an irremediable sense of dispersion. But I see people

living in real time who, as they perform their various operations, no longer have any identity problem and become, as a result, increasingly efficient, since, to play with the networks, to move from one part of the spectrum to the other, you don't need either to be yourself or to be free any longer (in this sense we're quite close to the logic of play); you have only to be ductile (docile), flexible and transparent.

You say, too, somewhere that real time doesn't exist. That real time never exists in the immediate term: all that's real is always deferred. (But perhaps that's a false quote too!)

We have to avoid the confusion of terms here. What's called 'real time' today is, in fact, the time of virtual reality, of the simultaneous screens and networks. It's the time, then, of an extreme simulation, that time precisely which, by contrast with traditional 'reality', can no longer admit of any difference within time.

Yes, the real doesn't, therefore, accept 'real time' as part of its make-up. If we speak of relative velocities, the real might perhaps be an effect of the slow-down of appearances. Meaning would be the world filtered through a slow-motion camera; simulation would be a form of acceleration; and integral reality a final form of the halting of the course of the world. (Although, as you say, 'speed and acceleration are merely the dream of making the world reversible'.) At any rate, it seems that these concepts which have been subjected to critique – identity, the principle of contradiction, which is geared to identity, transition, change, origin, end, substance, the social, which is a kind of broadening of the cogito *– can all be overturned as soon as we make a* *critique of time . . . Or the idea of substance: it's clear that it's geared to linearity. Time could be said to be the password that makes the reversion of these linear concepts possible, and it isn't possible to overturn these concepts and critique them without at the same time critiquing time or without indirectly rethinking time.*

Ultimately, you shouldn't really be able to abstract time or make it a transcendental dimension. Time is the very becoming of things; it isn't a kind of pre-existent temporal space that would merely be the dimension of their change or their succession. Similarly, language isn't a kind of material within which meaning would distribute itself: that's the language of communication, language as medium. But today, not just the time of becoming, but the very time of history come to grief in real time. Yet, nothing happens there, since in real time everything is over-exposed simultaneously.

The Abolition of Night

NOAILLES: *It's like that image you used: if the speed of light were infinite, all the stars would be there at once, and the incandescence would be unbearable.*

BAUDRILLARD: Yes, the space of the screen, of virtual reality, is the space of the abolition of night, the abolition of the alternation of night and day and of waking and dreaming – in a kind of perpetual watchfulness. One of the great differences between a future 'trans-realized' species and ourselves will be the definitive absence of night and dreaming. Now, consciousness exists only by passing from night to day, from sleep to waking.

Otherwise, it's eternal insomnia, a form of torture. We can imagine with a certain dread the sleepless nights in which whole armies would fight to get back to sleep. Chuang-Tzu and his butterfly come to mind here: was it Chuang-Tzu who dreamed he was a butterfly or the butterfly that dreamed it was Chuang-Tzu? If we had to find a sign that the universe had become unliveable, it would surely be the impossibility of continuing to ask this question. (Never being able to rest from oneself is the worst of hypotheses. Might that have happened to God? To indulge in more fantastical hypotheses of this kind, might God also be a victim of insomnia? Might we be the product of his insomnia rather than his dreams?) It's an abominable vision: we'd be a species akin to those battery hens who never see the light of day. The lights are permanently left on so that they lose all sense of time, so that they eat constantly and fatten up at great speed. This is how those hormone-inflated species grow, having never walked and never really been able to sleep.

The virtual beings of the future will be sleepless. Asexual and sleepless. Stanislaw Lec said: 'I had a dream about reality. It was such a relief to wake up.'[30] Well, the beings of the future, having lost sleep, won't even have the good fortune of dreaming of reality and escaping from it when they wake; they'll live perpetually in an integral reality, an integral daylight. This

---

[30] Stanislaw J. Lec, *Unkempt Thoughts* (New York: St Martin's Press, 1962), p. 154.

paradoxical shifting from dream to wakefulness, from night to day, this rhythm of transition from the one form to the other, this is roughly what the form of time is like – and it enables you, by alternation, to escape the unilateral reality principle.

Being incapable of crossing the fragile frontier between waking and sleep, will they in the end be beings without boundaries, living in the absolute desert of integral reality with no alternation? When you eliminate an aspect of the fundamental duality of the world – in this case, sleep – the surviving term suffers an equivalent death by hypertrophy. So we'd find ourselves facing a hypertrophy of wakefulness. We'd be faced with open eyes, but no waking state (as when Macedonio Fernandez writes: 'Not all is wakefulness in open eyes'). Just as not all is sleep in closed eyes.

Where substance and identity are concerned, a wonderful Nasreddin story comes to mind, the story of the cat and the pound of meat. The master, seeing that the meat has disappeared, questions the servant girl, who says the cat has eaten it. The master says: 'We'll see about that.' He has the cat weighed. It weighed a pound before and still weighs a pound. So, the master says, 'If that's the cat, where's the meat? If the meat's there, then where's the cat?' I would ask the same question in another connection. If you put the man who says he possesses the truth on the scales, and he weighs exactly what he did before, then if that's the man, where's the truth? If the truth is there, where's the man?

Perhaps illusion might be said to be a kind of dietetics. You should get your weight down!

Yes, I'm going to strive to spit out my truth, in order to preserve my waist-line. But watch out. If you make the cat spit the meat out, then there's no cat either! It's quite a business, this substitution of truth. Where it is, we are not. Where we are, it is not.

There's a fine ironic wisdom.

It's the idea that truth passes from one head to another, that substance passes from one form to another by a kind of prestidigitation, and that you can't anywhere say: 'That's the truth.'

It would be interesting to weigh thinkers after they've thought.

Yes, to measure the difference. As you see in the film '21 Grams', where the body loses 21 grams at the moment of death: it's the weight of the soul escaping. But, in a sense, this story of the subtraction of the meat or the truth is comforting, for if you take the truth away, what remains? The man remains, the human being, the singular being, who is never equivalent to truth, is never one with it. In even the most banal human beings there's a form irreducible to what they 'weigh', to any truth whatever or, indeed, to what they 'think', to the consciousness they have of themselves. A form of 'idiocy', as Clément Rosset would say.

It wouldn't be difficult to imagine which would be more dangerous, then, the claim to truth or absolute idiocy . . .

Quite obviously, truth. The truth is a dangerous madness, idiocy is merely a gentle madness. One can, admittedly, see madness as an idiomatic form, a singular form (Deleuze and schizophrenia). But, most of the time, madness is just the obverse of reason, as nonsense is just the obverse of sense or meaning. Being raving mad doesn't necessarily make you singular. Being unintelligible doesn't necessarily make you a genius. Madness is confused in the public imagination with unreason, with nonsense. It isn't, therefore, an alternative to truth (if there were one, it would be illusion, not unreason). But it doesn't have the form of singularity either.

It's a disturbance of the rules . . .

Exactly, whereas the symbolic form has a rule – it's the very opposite of a total deregulation. The problem was raised in the 1970s with regard to the concepts of de-territorialization of desire and its rhizomatic proliferation. We were, of course, all looking for a radical alternative. But rather than in a deregulation and a dissemination of desire, I saw that alternative in a set of rules of the symbolic game and a dual obligation. Deleuze talks a lot about becoming: becoming-animal, becoming-woman, becoming-child, etc. I find this form of becoming very fine, provided that it isn't confused with the proliferation of desire, which is merely the dispersal of a force. With the rhizome and the molecular, you find yourself faced with a constellation, an infinite host of possibilities. It's very poetic, but so far as this operation of multiplication to infinity and of de-territorialization is concerned, it happens to be the case that computers and all the new virtual technologies are carrying it out on a grand scale. It seemed to me that, in the guise of libidinal deregulation, Deleuze and Lyotard were simply ratifying the future state of things. As for Guattari's molecular revolution, I'm sorry, but it has, in a sense, become part of our lives – through genetics, computational biology, 'mental morphing', etc.

It's always the same thing: there's the conceptual moment, the moment of intuition and hypothesis, the philosophical moment, and then that tends to realize itself by every means possible. It's the aim of all technologies to operationalize things, including philosophical visions and insights.

Perhaps the strength of a thought is proportional to the impossibility of its realization? Might thought be a form of pure waste?

No, I don't think so. Writing's often portrayed today as a kind of potlatch or a sort of ready-made. But writing is an act of mastery, which conforms to the conditions of a managed intervention, but does so without a determinate project and without any illusions as to its general destination. Fortunately or unfortunately, others will seize on it and turn it into a discourse of truth, either to illustrate it or to criticize it. Inertia always operates in that direction – taking on truth, taking on reference, searching for signs and marks.

Yes, it's the eternal questions: 'Where are you coming from? Where are you going? What position do you speak from? Who authorizes you to do so? And, above all, who authorized you not to believe in the real?'

The moment of writing is transfused into the linear time of communication, of reception, diffusion and commentary . . . But one colludes in that too. Of course, you can try to escape it, but it's like trying to walk in the snow without leaving footprints.

Yes, so long as the snow hasn't melted! You say: 'No thought can be sure of itself nor conscious of its mechanism; it must espouse the risks of what it doesn't say and not the prudence of what it says.' In other words, there's a radicalism of thought when it doesn't aspire to prove itself. But you sometimes say it's a game we know the rules of. So I wonder about the 'innocence' of thought. You're lost if you know its mechanism . . .

If you know the instruction manual, yes. Then you become a kind of finite object for yourself. There are styles of writing, for example, that have no secret to them, where you see how they've been manufactured – like a technical object. But sometimes, in writing, you have the delightful impression that something has worked secretly, something unforeseeable, something you have no sight of. A secret which is, in the end, a bit like the secret of birth – your own birth remains forever a secret to you (your own death too).

Can there be said to be a 'consciousness' of the mechanism when, in order to speak of speed, you adopt a rapid form? When, to speak of seduction, language itself assumes that seductive form?

I'm not sure this collusion between thought and writing is a reflective form; it might, rather, be said to be a reflex form whereby language partakes of the event of thought by an unconscious strategy. At any rate, seduction, whatever the object of the discourse, is part of the originality of writing. It is, indeed, its original form.

If the operation of thought is homologous with the operation of the world (the best-case scenario), there's no strategy at all.

You're part of a strategy on the part of the world.

Of a strategy without a strategist. Of something, like thought in fact, that can barely be called strategic, since strategy presupposes an evaluation, a calculation, a choice of ends and means.

But in Fatal Strategies, *it doesn't work like that.*

That's right. But the term 'fatal strategy' has always been poorly understood. I've misused the term myself at times to refer to an irrational strategy that has disastrous consequences. A bad decision, as it were . . . whereas a fatal strategy is something quite different: it's the invention of a destiny. That is to say, an undertaking in which an involuntary reversibility is in play, for better or for worse. One in which striving for one's ends drags you irresistibly in the opposite direction; or, alternatively, one in which not striving for your ends gets you to them without your wanting to. There is in it, at any rate, an outstripping of any will of your own. Seduction, for example, is a fatal strategy. But if you conceive it in terms of calculation and manipulation (for sexual or other ends), you sink into a banal strategy in the most vulgar sense.

Here, the example of Kierkegaard's seducer . . .

. . . is quite remarkable because he, precisely, sees himself as effecting such a deliberate strategy, yet it's he, in the end, who's caught in the trap: he forgot that seduction is *fatal* or, in other words, reversible.

He's within a game that's bigger than he is.

Yes, and if the hero doesn't know this, Kierkegaard certainly does. He describes with precision the unilateral strategy of the person who tries to boss the game, but he knows the game has no boss, that no one can be bigger than the game itself.

You think you control the game, whereas the game controls you.

It's the illusion of the will. Or even, in the case of the 'dice man', the illusion of the 'will to chance'.[31] According to what may seem a fatal strategy, the dice man chooses to entrust his fate at any moment to the random decision of the dice, that is to say, to a random operation of desire – a challenge to his ego and to his own will. In a sense, then, he's trying to be master of the game of chance. But he fails totally – chance (which doesn't exist, having, *pace* Mallarmé, been abolished long ago) propels him back inexorably to his own desire.

---

[31] The allusion is to Luke Rhinehart's novel, *The Dice Man* (London: Panther, 1972).

But the trap of seduction – and even the trap of Kierkegaard's story – is that, in the first instance, people feel capable of producing it.

Unlike the Don Juans and Casanovas – and far superior to them in this respect – Kierkegaard, through his character Johannes, carries out a very thorough experimental study of this strategic logic. It's by pushing this kind of undertaking, which is independent of desire, to its logical end that he shows that the subject of seduction transforms himself imperceptibly into a victim, and that there is, then, no subject of seduction, but a division of roles.

When all's said and done, the only thing you can produce is a vacuum, an irresistible zone of attraction into which things tend to fall, to plunge. It's as if you were satisfying this secret desire of things.

Yes, that is Johannes's tactic – almost the tactic of an oriental martial art. And that's doubtless also Kierkegaard's relation to his own writing. He too inevitably succumbs to the seduction of the text, while exerting that seduction. In writing, too, you are always both master and victim.

From time to time, there's a happy coincidence, the charm of a certain predestination where a number of things intersect. An actual grace, but a grace that may veer towards madness.

A Luxurious Dysfunction

NOAILLES: *You sometimes seem to come to the same conclusion as Sartre: thought is, ultimately, a useless passion. In Sartre there was something nostalgic in that judgement. It's as though one were saying, 'After so much effort, it's useless!' Whereas, in this case, it's something different! It's before any effort that it's useless, and it's perhaps only for that reason that one does it . . .*

BAUDRILLARD: Useless for what? We always say things are useful for something, but what are they useless for?

Useless in the sense that this stage of the virtual can be said to have entirely cleared the way for thought at last to be free to be useless.

Right. And at that point it becomes a passion again, since it's only in uselessness that something like a passion functions. As a result, it returns the virtual, which is monopolizing all useful functions, to its uselessness.

Perhaps, then, it's the new – necessarily useless – passion?

It isn't uselessness that defines passion. Thought as passion could be described like this: when energy is straining towards an end and that end disappears, then the potential energy passes into a phase in which it has no meaning, but all the more intensity for that. The end is lost, but the intensity remains, which can then transfer itself to language and writing. But, unless it's shared, thought, when freed entirely from its ends, can quite simply turn to paranoia. However, uselessness isn't the essential thing – it's a prior condition or a secondary determination. For example, art, that other useless passion, isn't useless in itself, if I can put it that way. It's useless additionally; it's beyond usefulness and uselessness. Unfortunately, it doesn't remain in that sublime zone: from the nineteenth century onwards, it aspires to be useless, it plays at the uselessness of 'art for art' and at that point it sinks into aesthetics.

Would that mean that thought is a luxurious dysfunction?

Dysfunctioning is in itself more entertaining than functioning, but, ultimately, we can say that the dysfunction is a variant – and perhaps the most successful variant – of functioning, that inadaptation is the most successful form of adaptation, etc. Things are more complicated today, because the fact of dysfunctioning is part of the game. Everyone's required to be different, singular, anomic, subversive. And even disablement is a bonus. There's a whole paranormal conformism going on.

Can you give an example of this injunction?

The whole of advertising today has as its leitmotif irony, transgression, and the interplay of prohibition and its overstepping. According to Philippe Muray, the 'festive' is our new categorical imperative – deregulation in partying.

Casting off responsibility?

Yes, obeying the pleasure principle, no longer genuflecting to the reality principle. Everything becomes an opportunity for a big parade, a great collective show in the new spaces of freedom. That is, of course, all of the order of duty and morality, and has nothing to do with that luxurious dysfunction we were talking about.

How to Eat the Nothing?

NOAILLES: *I'd like to introduce another fake quotation now: 'Keyboard not found. Press any key to continue.' This could well be from Genesis (or even from the book of Revelation). And I'd like us to speak about the problem of nihilism, of the nothing and the continuation of the nothing. It seems that nihilism is an immense surgical procedure carried out on the nothing, aimed at radically extirpating it. According to Heidegger, nihilism is the forgetting of the nothing: perhaps the essence of nihilism lies in not taking the question of nothingness seriously . . . 'What are we to say, then, if the omission of this question regarding the essence of nothingness was the reason why Western metaphysics has fallen into nihilism?' he asks. Nietzsche, it seems to me, is different because, in his view, nihilism is the devaluing of all values and the triumph of the reactive forces. And Heidegger says further: 'How does it come about that being has primacy everywhere and claims for itself all that "is", whereas what is not an essent, the nothing understood as Being itself, is forgotten?' We might wonder, then, whether true nihilism wouldn't be to forget the nothing by material-*

izing it in the essent. Nihilism might be said to be the systematic elimination of the nothing in the analysis of things.

BAUDRILLARD: But we should differentiate the nothing from that which is worthless (*nul*) – by maintaining the idea that what is worthless is precisely that which has forgotten the nothing. You see this in great systems like political economy, which is based ultimately on the exchange of the nothing, on the multiplication of zero-sum exchanges. Exchange is exchange for the nothing, and it's the nothing that's exchanged beneath the apparent exchange of value. We have here the twofold aspect of impossible exchange. In the interstices of exchanges squints the nothing, and we squint at the nothing (convergent strabismus). Most of the time, it's worthlessness that rules, the equivalence of the nothing. But, from time to time, the nothing draws attention to itself as what it 'is'; the absent term of every exchange resurfaces in the breakdown, the accident, the crisis of generalized exchange.

We may note two things, then. Everything is exchanged for nothing – this is 'traditional' nihilism. By contrast, nothing is exchanged, the nothing is inexchangeable – this is impossible exchange, though here we have the superlative dimension, the poetic dimension of impossible exchange. This is the opposite of nihilism. It's the resurgence of the nothing at the heart of the essent, at the heart of the something. Warhol talked, for example, of bringing out the nothingness at the heart of the image. And Barthes's *punctum* in photography is this too: the blind spot, the non-place at the heart of the image. What, then, would the opposite of nihilism be?

Duality perhaps. That which leaves the dual principle of things intact, and isn't intent on exterminating the nothing.

I entirely agree. It's the dual form that creates the void and preserves the void, whereas oneness, being always the oneness of the whole, of the something, no longer leaves space for the nothing. Antonio Machado says that we always credit God with having created the world *ex nihilo*, with having created something out of nothing, but we ought to acknowledge in him a much higher power, that of having created nothingness out of something.

Yes, and we could perhaps draw here on the story of the worm that ate its parasite, even though it was vital to it. At some point, we really did eat the nothing; we made it disappear and realized the world completely.

We've filled up the world, yes. We've eaten the nothing. The image is a fine one.

The nothing as the parasite that enables you to digest the real. Having devoured that parasite, we can no longer digest the real. That's why reality is so heavy. And perhaps illusion doesn't eat the real because that would also spell its own death.

We could go back here to the story of Kant's dove which, feeling the resistance of the wind, imagines it would fly much faster in a vacuum. So we imagine we'll arrive at absolute Good if we eliminate Evil, at the All if we eliminate the Nothing, at the Eternal if we eliminate Time. We conceive the Nothing as a diabolic resistance and as an emanation of Evil. A total misconception – the Nothing is as essential to life as are air and wind to the flight of the dove. The proof is in the cruel Bible saying, 'He that hath not, from him shall be taken even that which he hath.'[32]

Let's go back to the question of nihilism. In the Heideggerian version, it's the forgetting of the nothing, and hence its exclusion. In the Nietzschean version, that of active nihilism, it might be said to mean pushing things, value systems, to their limits, where it turns out that there's nothing, that they lead to nothing. It is, all the same, a way of making the nothing appear in the end – a sort of forceps delivery. But once again, we have to distinguish between the two, between the positive and negative connotations of the nothing. This ambivalence is, to some degree, the ambivalence we find with the remainder. The remainder and the nothing are somehow linked. 'Of the remainder' – and I'm not playing on words here – once the operation is finished, 'nothing remains'. That is to say, when the world is completed, it's the nothing that remains. The very term [*rien*, in French] is etymologically ambiguous, since it comes from *rerum*, which means 'something'.[33]

We could also come at this subject from the angle of your question: 'Why is there nothing rather than something?' with the nothing 'positively' connoted. It's more or less what Gorgias says. We have, as it were, run through his treatise On the Nonexistent or On Nature[34] *in both directions: being is not; if it were, it would be unknowable; and if it were knowable, it would be inexpressible. History has travelled the journey that leads from the constating of being to the accreditation of the knowledge of being and the creation of the subject that expresses it. In our turn, by rapidly travelling the*

---

[32] Mark 4: 25.
[33] The derivation of *rien* is more conventionally given from the accusative singular, *rem*.
[34] This is known also as *On Non-Being or On Nature*.

opposite path, we've devoured that history . . . by beginning at the end: we've rid ourselves of the subject of knowledge, we've rid ourselves of knowledge itself, and we've come back to the initial finding, this time in its 'negative' sense.

Yes, we're devouring history, this time retrospectively. For so long as it was unfolding, we could retain the illusion of understanding it. Today, it's coming to an end without our knowing why. We're trying, therefore, to revive it, so as to guess its meaning, to 'digest' it. It's the same as with the Big Bang. We have perpetually to go back to it to try to understand what there was *before* – that is to say, Nothing. It's hopeless. With the Nothing, we're in initial despair and, with the obliteration of history, in final despair.

You've spoken of things like that: the nihilism of transparency or, in other words, the process of the destruction of appearances in favour of meaning.

Yes, it's the temptation to reduce duality; the lethal temptation to reunify the whole, with the nothing eliminated.

One might think the nothing is what protects things from becoming something, and thus from coming to an end, for when they realize themselves, that's also their end. This functions then a bit like the theorem of the 'accursed share', doesn't it? When you take away all the viruses, the antibodies have nothing to do.

Yes, we've devoured the accursed share. Since appearances are what protect us from reality, to arrive at integral reality, appearances and their symbolic envelope have to be abolished. Reality devours appearances the way the worm devours its parasite, and integral reality devours them integrally.

But illusion remains intact, like Jonah inside a double whale!

We may take the view, too, that it's illusion, with its veils, that protects us from naked reality.

You say, 'It would be fine to be a nihilist if there were still a radicality!' And they continue to accuse you of nihilism!

Yes, and why not also of negationism?[35] Whereas it's the system that's truly negationist, since it's the denial of the nothing, the denial of any illusion. It's the whole system that's become nihilistic. Extending its moral nihilism, it's become technically nihilistic. And, as a result, the term no longer means much. Nihilism (which is the forgetting of the nothing) is technically realized. Having said that, we always hear the same test-of-confidence question: where does all that get you? The old ultimatum, the old ideology of a reconciliation of theory and practice, the old dialectical nostalgia – of the kind we've absorbed throughout our philosophical and moral education! It's

---

[35] The French term 'négationnisme' generally denotes 'Holocaust denial'. It is, of course, used more broadly here, but the negative connotations are still present.

incredible how encrusted this prejudice for reality is, not just in people's practice, but in their imaginations. I believe it to be insurmountable. It's the easiest solution, as Lichtenberg says. Hence it's the one with the brightest future.

How can we take this kind of analysis to the other side (not the side of reality of course) without debasing it completely? How can we recover a dual relation on the basis of practical uselessness? In a word, is there, all the same, a possible exchange of impossible exchange?

And why is there a kind of basic temptation here? Is it perhaps the temptation of things to be always outside of themselves . . .

Well, I'm beside myself in every sense of the word!

This drive everything has – perhaps it's the will to power after all . . . (the will not being what people will, but that which wills in willing, as Deleuze says). Perhaps the will to power is not just a will of things to grow, but pure superhuman desire, the pure desire of things or that of immanence, at a particular moment, to become an ecstasy – not the ecstasy of simulation which you describe, but rather the opposite: 'ek-stasis' in the etymological sense. Even illusion wouldn't resist . . .

It's its destiny to exorcise itself, as it were.

To extricate itself, to de-realize itself.

Extricating itself, de-realizing itself – this is a fatal hypothesis. The banal strategy being that which wishes simply to externalize itself, to expose itself so as to realize itself. Over against that, there's the strategy that puts itself dramatically in play, so as not to realize itself. At the cost of disappearing even, for there's a subtle difficulty in coming out of oneself while avoiding realizing oneself. It's a little bit like this with writing. Something finds its ultimate form, always slightly short of its realization. You have, in this way, to keep your balance in the paroxystic moment.

That's a fantastic idea! A challenge you can't shirk, but one that has to be stopped in time, on pain of disappearance. It would be an ek-stasis that never gets to stasis; illusion that opens up and closes again at the same time. Like the paroxysm, which stops before the end, what would be the term to refer to what stops before the beginning? A world that won't fulfill all its possibilities, and that never opens its umbrella either . . . In reality, we can't dismiss the fact that, when you walk, the path moves too. The forward march of the world creates a similar effect of advancement: you don't leave the spot because the path moves in step with you. There's a very subtle movement here between immobility and the first step; the world can almost never be said to have taken the first step . . .

In any event, we never knew it. But we can imagine the last.

All in all, what would never have taken a first step is the world as radical illusion. Appearances are there, but they'd never succeed in taking a step beyond themselves. The first step is signification and meaning; that is to say, the first step is always the one that leads to the abyss. The Big Bang, the realization of the world would include the simultaneous triggering of the Big Crunch. As you said, the two processes get under way at the same time.

Thought is produced by the ecstasy of the world itself: it's part of its unfolding, its dispersal, at the same time as it's the distillation of the world in homeopathic doses. In this sense, the history of the universe is thrilling. This universe born of the expanding Big Bang, but not seeing itself, since there isn't any light yet, and hence not having the possibility of reflecting [on] itself. Then light appears and hence visibility, but there's no one to see. Then life appears, and hence something that can see. And lastly thought, which reflects the whole. But that's doubtless not the end-point. One is always tempted to loop back on this course of events.

That's interesting because I've always loved the fact that there are insects on the sea bottom, in a place of total darkness, and that they have extraordinary colours. A useless beauty that will never be seen. A beauty unconcerned with being seen . . .

The opposite would be the pure gaze, without there being anything to see . . . A useless function . . . the function of God.

A fine expression . . . We find the opposite image in the other excess, in the hyperreality of those images to which people lend attention but which offer nothing to the gaze, in the obscenity in which the distance of the gaze disappears, in the form of gaze that has closed the circle so as to have nothing to see either . . .

But I've another underwater story. It's the story of a deep-sea creature with a minimal brain, which wanders around for a long time before finding a spot to which to affix itself. As soon as it's found one, it survives by devouring itself. And what it devours first is its own brain.[36] This modicum of grey matter that served only to help it find its place is no longer needed, so it devours it. I wonder whether the human race isn't following the same course.

First of all, I like these 'scientific' examples, which are heirs, in a sense, to simulation, and which one can take up as though they were illusions, too . . . When science sometimes has these kinds of intuitions, it recoils from them. Ernst Mach, who straddled philosophy and physics, saw the universe as a 'one-sided entity, whose mirror complement does not exist or, at least, is not known to us'. He initially opts for a form of impossible exchange, but he steps back just in time, leaving a door open to the possibility that the universe can acquire value! In any event, your underwater story's a troubling allegory . . . (Can we imagine a species that would have found an allegory of its end that was so fine that it couldn't resist the fate of bringing it to fruition? A species whose destiny would have been entirely bewitched by a little story?) But would that species, like the sea-creature, have found the fixed point that enables it to devour its singularity?

Endowed with a superior intelligence, which has perhaps enabled it to find its place, the human race is devouring it. It's using its brain as an operational mechanism to the point of sacrificing it to artificial intelligence. There it is in its fixed spot. The operation's over. It's come to its end. And so it devours its own thought, that function that has now become useless. The species, having arrived at its ends, gives up on itself and its own specificity.

---

[36] The reference is to the sea-squirt, which, at a certain point in its life cycle, digests its own cerebral ganglion.

Yes, or perhaps we've gone even further. Perhaps we've succeeded in throwing off, in some unthought-out way, this fixed point that prompted us to devour ourselves, and are now lost in indefinite seriality, in an inertia devoid of any reference. It's interesting: if human beings find a fixed spot, a point of reference, they devour themselves. If they completely lose that fixed point, they remain 'freed' from themselves and are exposed to a kind of metastasis. Might there be an intermediate strategy, a form that combines the attempt at preservation, which a fixed point of purchase implies, and the attempt at abandonment that leads to their final doom?

The destiny of thought is that of the species. And that destiny lies within its singular limit. In other words, thought must never devour the distance that separates it from itself. It must always be exiled from itself (and 'exiled from dialogue'!). Or, to put it another way, it cannot, except by abolishing itself, jump over its shadow and into transparency. It cannot immortalize itself before the mirror of truth, which reflects back only its own image. There's a horizon of thought, which is pushed back as it goes along and which it must never reach. That is the very horizon, the uncrossable horizon, of singularity. This is, literally, the meaning of aphorism – *aphorizein*: the end-point, the limit of a process, be it thought or writing, that will never reach its end. By contrast, the virtual might be said rather to map out the hypochondriacal field of a thought obsessed by its own functioning, absorbing its own limits and its own horizon. The species itself has this same configuration. It too can't jump over its shadow without destroying itself. It too, unless it is to destroy itself, has to keep within the limits of an inescapable singularity, where it will have an infinite spread spectrum available to it.